A History of SURBITON GOLF CLUB

by

Malcolm W. H. Peebles

Printed by
Kelsi Print (Fulham) Limited
Feltham, Middlesex

Previous books by the author:

— Evolution of the Gas Industry, The Macmillan Press Ltd., 1980.
— The Claygate Book: a History of a Surrey Village, Peebles, 1983.

A HISTORY OF SURBITON GOLF CLUB

First published 1987 by Malcolm Peebles, Claygate, Surrey.

Printed by Kelsi Print (Fulham) Limited, Felthambrook, Feltham, Middlesex.

British Library Cataloguing in Publication Data

Peebles, Malcolm W. H.
A History of Surbiton Golf Club.
1. Surbiton Golf Club - History
I. Title
796.352'06'042194 GV969.S9
ISBN 0-9508978-1-7

CONTENTS

DEDICATION

Freddie Pyrke

This book is dedicated to Freddie Pyrke, Captain of Surbiton Golf Club from June 1955 to June 1957, to his Committees, Sub-Committees and helpers, to the Club's Secretary of that time, Ernie Newman, and not least of all, to those 'A' and 'B' Notes subscribers who pledged monies to the Club in those tumultuous days of the Club's history when very nearly all was lost.

But it is to Freddie Pyrke in particular that this dedication is made. It was he more than any other individual who fought tooth and nail to keep the Club alive as will become apparent later. Suffice it to say at this point that the sheer volume of letters he wrote and answered, the number of meetings he attended and the time he spent inspiring, discussing, cajoling and negotiating with folk, added up to a great many hours every day over a period of many months; a less determined man might well have thrown in the towel at a much earlier stage.

Freddie was born in 1901 and joined the Club in 1940. At his peak Freddie Pyrke played to a handicap of 10. By profession he was a Company Secretary; he died in 1985 and his ashes were scattered at Rectory Lane Cemetery, Long Ditton. A great servant of the Club to whom all members of the Club past and present owe an enduring debt of gratitude. His wife, Marion, was Ladies' Captain in 1957, and his son, Timothy, continues the family connection with the Club today.

In conclusion, the selection of any one individual among so many members who have served the Club in a wide variety of ways over the last ninety years is always open to some criticism and alternative suggestions. I hope that in this instance the majority will agree that while Freddie Pyrke may well have had some peers, there is no-one in living memory who has exceeded his contribution in a tangible sense. To repeat, in making this dedication I couple with his name all those who in their various ways helped to save the Club for future generations in 1956/57.

Malcolm Peebles
May 1987

FOREWORD

Gilbert Fuge

It is an especial privilege to have been asked to write a Foreword for this book.

Disraeli said, 'Never take anything for granted', but, of course, we all do. We may be members of Surbiton Golf Club, but I wonder if we ever pause to appreciate its interesting and enjoyable features or stop to reflect that it takes careful thought, skilful planning, and a great deal of effort to preserve the Club that gives us a great deal of pleasure.

The preparation of this fascinating account of our history will I am sure bring pleasure to the members and friends of the Club, will re-kindle memories of the older folk and stimulate the interest of the young.

'Our History' is the product of many minds and it would be invidious to select names for mention, but a deserved exception must be made for Malcolm Peebles whose dedication has been the driving force behind the publication. To him and to all who helped in the research, writing, illustrating, editing and production, we give grateful thanks.

During this period of declining standards in the way of life, and attitudes of both participants and spectators in all forms of sport, I am hopeful that 'Our History' will make all members and friends (past, present and future) aware of our traditions and standards, and the continual need to uphold these to protect a most wonderful and friendly Club that we own in its entirety.

We must all seek to preserve and enhance all that is best in our Club heritage.

Gilbert F. Fuge.

G. F. Fuge, O.B.E.
Captain 1985/86
Director & Chairman,
Surbiton Golf Club Ltd. from 1984
Trustee 1971–84
Committee Member 1976–79

INTRODUCTION

O wad some Pow'r the giftie gie us
To see oursels as others see us!

So Robert Burns exclaimed as he observed the illicit progress of a louse over a lady's bonnet. Many golfers must secretly wish that they too could be given the gift of seeing themselves as others see them as they endeavour to strike that infuriating little ball with their inadequate, misshapen implements that the Rules of Golf permit us to use. And so it is, in some respects, when one attempts to write a history of Surbiton Golf Club – more a potpourri of peoples' impressions, opinions and recollections, than a wealth of concrete facts recounted objectively and with precision.

At the request of the then Captain, Gilbert Fuge, I embarked on this task in the autumn of 1985. It quickly became apparent that due to three fires in earlier years, and probably successive clear-outs by some past Secretaries, there was very little material of a historic factual nature in the Club's archives to research. Much, therefore, that is recorded in this book has been gleaned from the memories of a relatively few Club members, who have at the same time made it clear to me that memories can and do falter with the passage of time. Moreover, given the Laws of Nature, it is not possible to go back much farther in time than the 1930s as far as this particular source of material is concerned. This is not to say that the Club's early years are a total mystery and have gone by default, but simply to explain to the reader that there are inevitable gaps and, quite possibly, some inaccuracies in what has been recorded. Even as far as more recent years are concerned, one can be almost certain that there will be some significant omissions of events and personalities which will come to light after publication.

All these qualifications having been made, it is nevertheless hoped that the reader will find something in this book that is new and of interest to him or her. If nothing else, perhaps this book will serve as a basis for some others to research and write a more detailed account in years to come.

To revert to Burns's quotation, a club, by definition, is a 'group or association of people with common aims or interests'. It is the nature and mix of men and women, not so much the golf course itself or the

Club's facilities, that makes Surbiton Golf Club what it is at any point of time. Some older members have indicated that the character of the Club has changed since they first joined it; some say for the better, some say for the worse, it is all a matter of individual taste and perception – seeing ourselves as others see us, so to speak.

Undoubtedly, the character of the Club, as well as its more tangible assets, will continue to change as its membership changes and as the general pattern of life exerts its influence. Within the membership time of many existing post-war members, substantial changes have already occurred, some in spite of considerable resistance at the time they were proposed. In twenty years, or more, or less, hence, Surbiton Golf Club may bear little resemblance to the Club we know today. One could speculate what these changes might be, but let us leave that to future historians to record and come back to the matter in hand which is the past, not the future.

Surbiton Golf Club, Thursday 12th June, 1986

SEASIDE GOLF

by

John Betjeman

How straight it flew, how long it flew,
   It clear'd the rutty track
And soaring, disappeared from view
   Beyond the bunker's back –
A glorious, sailing, bounding drive
That made me glad I was alive.

And down the fairway, far along
   It glowed a lonely white;
I played an iron sure and strong
And clipp'd it out of sight,
And spite of grassy banks between
I knew I'd find it on the green.

And so I did. It lay content
   Two paces from the pin;
A steady putt and then it went
   Oh, most securely in.
The very turf rejoiced to see
That quite unprecedented three.

ACKNOWLEDGEMENTS

I wish to express my gratitude to all those members and staff of Surbiton Golf Club whose interest, encouragement, personal contributions and practical assistance have helped to make this book possible.

Among the many contributions I received, I should particularly like to thank Walter Bradley for his very extensive recollections stretching back over many years which gave me many valuable clues and pointers for further research and investigation. To his name I wish to couple those of Pip Whitehorn, Doris Hynes, Tim Pyrke, Dick Hall, Percy Beer, Alastair Craig, Bill Farenden, Madge Picknett, David Randall and others who scratched their memories and volunteered many details of the Club relating to its earlier years.

My special thanks are also due to Anne Biggs and Karen Wilson for their excellent and patient typing of my hand-written manuscript. And also to Don Blanchard and Gilbert Fuge who kindly read all my drafts to ensure, to the best of their ability and knowledge, that what is recorded herein contains no glaring errors or unfortunate misrepresentations.

In addition, a number of organisations have kindly responded to my enquiries and have provided me with information, while several publishers have readily given their permission to quote extracts from their books and journals. Their ready co-operation in these matters has been of considerable practical and factual assistance. Finally, these acknowledgements would not be complete without an expression of thanks to Mike Wright, the Club's Secretary/Manager, who I pestered with many queries and requests which he handled with unfailing courtesy, and to David Redpath and Colin Philimore (of Kelsi Print) who kindly arranged the printing of this book.

Lastly, most of the illustrations in this book have been provided by Club members - my thanks to them for this, also to Chris Riley who masterminded reproduction of them for me.

This book has been a personal project and as such does not purport to represent the Club's official history but simply my own version of it. If because of any inaccuracies, omissions, or unsought for inclusions herein I have inadvertently caused possible embarrassment to any persons, I trust they will accept my sincere apologies.

The author, May 1987

CHAPTER 1

THE ORIGIN OF SURBITON GOLF CLUB

The Club owes its existence in the first instance to the financial generosity and enthusiasm for golf of Mr. A. H. Lisner of The Waffrons, Long Ditton, and of 119 Pall Mall, London, while in later years others were to save the Club from extinction as will become clear.

The Founding of the Waffrons Golf Club

In the 'Surrey Comet' of Saturday 9th March, 1895, it was reported that Mr. A. H. Lisner, the lessee of The Waffrons and its farmland, was proposing to lay down a golf course on old pastures surrounding the farmhouse. He had had the ground surveyed by the professional golfer and golf course architect, Tom Dunn, who had stated in his report '. . . *that the land and turf were well adapted to this purpose, capable of providing a long and good nine-hole course fully a mile and a half in length, possessing the great recommendation of natural hazards*'. Mr. Lisner said that in the event of a sufficient number of prospective members coming forward, he would personally pay to lay down and keep in order the course, erect a clubhouse for the use of subscribers, engage a professional, and even go as far as to provide conveyance to the ground for members living in Surbiton, Kingston, the Dittons, Esher and Molesey. In all probability, the first 50 members would be admitted without entrance fee. It was claimed that numerous promises of support had already been received. It was further stated that '. . . *the liability of each member would be limited to the amount of the annual subscription, which will be kept as moderate a figure as is compatible with the desire that the club shall be both popular and select.*'

Letters to the 'Surrey Comet' during the following week included:

> '*A more suitable locality would be difficult to find . . . the proposed club cannot fail to be a success . . . Saturdays and Sundays will no doubt be reserved for gentlemen players*'.
>
> *(Signed) 'Bunker' of Regent's Park.*

and

'. . . no time should be lost in laying out the course and getting the ground into good order . . .'

(Signed) Colonel 'Bogey'

Meanwhile, competition for members appeared with the announcement that Claygate Common Golf Course was to be opened on 1st May, 1895. This was a nine-hole course laid out by Pinkerton, the Guildford Club professional, which covered nearly 1½ miles and claimed to be *'a good sporting course with plenty of natural hazards'*. This club prospered until the beginning of the Great War; shortly thereafter the club was wound up and the course reverted to common land. The land in question is that which lies to the south of Common Road, Claygate, and is today known as Claygate Common.

On 23rd March, 1895, the following advertisement appeared in the 'Surrey Comet':

TO GOLFERS

A MEETING of GOLFERS and prospective players will be held at the SOUTHAMPTON HOTEL, SURBITON, on FRIDAY NEXT, the 29th March, at 6 p.m. for the purpose of forming a GOLF CLUB to play upon the links about to be laid down at THE WAFFRONS, UPPER LONG DITTON.

Numerous applications for membership have already been received from ladies and gentlemen in the neighbourhood, but all who are interested in the game are cordially invited to attend.

A provisional Committee will probably be elected at the meeting.

A. H. Lisner
The Waffrons
Upper Long Ditton.

The meeting was duly held and presided over by Mr. Bulmer Howell who subsequently became the Club's first Captain. There was a good attendance of the gentry, while Lisner told the meeting that he had 70 names of ladies and gentlemen wishing to join. Howell said that he preferred the club not to be a proprietary one, but he was afraid there would be insuperable difficulties in the way of placing it on any other basis. A provisional Committee was elected, but their names are not recorded as the press were asked to withdraw at this point.

Things moved very quickly after this: The Waffrons Golf Club was formally instituted in April 1895, the course (nine holes) was ready for play on Saturday 18th May, 1895, while a 'handsome and commodious' clubhouse was already under construction.

The fact that the course was ready for play so soon, is probably accounted for by the fact that some years earlier the Ritchie family, who then occupied The Waffrons as, I believe, tenants of Lisner, had laid out a rudimentary course for the benefit of the sons of the family, Frank and James Ritchie. Presumably, the course architect, Tom Dunn, made the most of this when designing and constructing the new course for the Club.

The Official Opening

The official opening of The Waffrons Golf Club was on Saturday 8th June, 1895, and the celebrations included an 18 hole competition in which eighteen members participated. It was won by James Wild with a net score of 78 (gross 94).

A press report of that time states:

> *The links to which there is a delightful carriage drive, are admirably situated; they command wide sweeps of some lovely scenery and are at the same time charmingly secluded. A handsome pavilion has been erected, and is being fitted with every convenience . . . the greens compare favourably with any in the country. It is proposed to run a conveyance between Surbiton and the grounds at stated times, commencing Saturday the 29th inst. . . . The membership of the Club numbers over a hundred of the best of the neighbouring society, and a few more will be elected without an entrance fee.*

The promise of the conveyance was kept. This was a break – an open, four-wheeled, horse-drawn carriage – accommodating ten, from Surbiton station at 4.50 p.m. after the arrival of the 4.20 p.m. train from Waterloo, leaving the Club on its return journey to Surbiton at 7 p.m. The first trip was made on 29th June, 1895.

The first Autumn Meeting was held on Saturday 26th October, 1895, when the principal competition resulted in a tie between Bulmer Howell and William Wood-Smith. Scores were:

B. Howell	81 scr. = 81	Rev. A. E. Bevan	129–26 = 103
W. Wood-Smith	105–24 = 81	J. C. Mewburn	136–30 = 106
W. Carr	87 scr. = 87	J. W. Dickinson	135–24 = 111
H. A. Perkin	109–15 = 94	R. Mould	152–30 = 122
J. D. Cowan	126–24 = 102	S. Ellson	156–30 = 126

A Change of Name

At the Club's second Annual General Meeting on Saturday 16th May, 1896, which was also the second day of the Club's first two-day Spring Meeting, Lisner informed the meeting that he had acquired 40 acres of meadow at the Claygate end of the links, and it was proposed to increase the number of holes from 9 to 18 as soon as the land could be prepared for this purpose; this was expected to be from October that year. Members present were:

Atkinson	G. J. Ingram
J. W. Dickinson	W. E. James
V. N. Douetil	W. Ford-Lewis
C. H. Evans	A. H. Lisner
S. Ellson	J. C. Mewburn
E. Evershed	R. Mould
A. C. Fairbairn	A. Nisbet
P. L. Foxwell	F. B. Norris
T. Gourley	H. Wood-Smith
E. Hall	A. B. Tomkins
E. C. Haram	G. T. Wrench

In the absence of the Captain, Bulmer Howell, Victor Douetil was voted to the Chair; H. E. Walton was Secretary.

At this meeting it was agreed to increase the membership limit from 200 to 400 as soon as 18 holes were available (actual membership in May 1896 was 130), and to increase the Committee from 6 to 15. Mr. Atkinson complained that the caddies were inefficient and inattentive, and suggested that the pro should train them, for which service he should retain one penny of the six pennies per round paid to the caddies.

The most important motion put to, and passed by, the meeting was that the name of the Club should be changed from The Waffrons to Surbiton Golf Club because '... *so few people know where The Waffrons was* ...'. Shortly after this meeting Lisner had the following notice printed and distributed to possible prospective members, a framed copy of which hangs today in the clubhouse. (See p.5).

Why Surbiton?

The popular speculation is that the appellation, Surbiton, was chosen because it had a certain snob appeal in view of its widely-held reputation as a high-class residential area; this was especially true in the second half of the nineteenth century and the earlier part of this century. Surbiton still possesses many grand houses, but most of these have now been converted into flats, or into nursing homes, schools, offices and such like; many others, of course, have been demolished

THE SURBITON GOLF CLUB
(late The Waffrons)

COMMITTEE

W. Carr | *E. R. Shipton*
C. W. Emson | *A. Mays-Smith*
B. Howell | *H. Wood-Smith*
W. Ford-Lewis | *A. H. Stoneham*
A. H. Lisner

The links are situated in one of the prettiest spots in Surrey, from whence views are obtained over several counties. They are approached (1) from Woodstock Lane, on the Surbiton-Claygate Road; (2) from the Portsmouth Road (Giggs Hill Green), where the Omnibus between Kingston, Surbiton and Esher passes each way every half-hour (only six minutes walk from the Omnibus to the links); (3) from Claygate by the footpath leading to Thames Ditton. Claygate is one mile distant, Surbiton two miles. When the second nine holes are opened (in September or October next), the course will come still nearer to Claygate station, on the Guildford line.

The Club was started a year ago, and numbers now about 130 members.

A large Pavilion has been erected, where Refreshments, Luncheons, etc, are provided.

Yearly subscription – 3 guineas Gentlemen, 1½ guineas Ladies.

Temporary Residents and Visitors in the neighbourhood can join for 2 guineas, covering the period from 1st May to 31st October; or at 5s per week.

Applications for further particulars, list of members, and forms of proposal to be addressed to

A. H. Lisner
The Waffrons
Long Ditton, Surbiton

May 1896

and replaced with more modest dwellings that better suit modern-day living, while the reputation that Surbiton enjoyed in the past has perhaps become attached to other locations such as Esher, Cobham and so on. An alternative more mundane explanation is that Surbiton was chosen simply because this was where most of the original Club members lived.

Many visitors must find the name rather confusing, given the Club's distance from Surbiton, its proximity to Claygate, and its Chessington postal address. But as it is called Surbiton, and probably will always bear that name, a few words on the origin of Surbiton may be appropriate at this point.

Until 1838, Surbiton was barely a hamlet in this remote and sparsely populated corner of Kingston parish. What brought it to life and subsequent prominence was the building of the Nine Elms and Woking railway, later to become the London and South Western Railway. This was planned to have run through Kingston, but the Borough of Kingston opposed this in a vain attempt to protect its then thriving coach trade – all to no avail as became apparent within a few years. With the coming of the railway, Surbiton grew very rapidly to reach a population of 15,000 by 1901. Meantime, Kingston was eventually obliged to accept the inevitable and obtained its own branch railway line in 1863.

Going back much farther in time, Surbiton derived the prefix of its name because it lay south (sur) of the Hogsmill River, and Norbiton because it was north (nor) of this river: the suffix 'biton' is derived from the word 'beretun' meaning an outlying grange, in both these instances of the Manor of Kingston. So much for the origins of the Club's name and that of Surbiton itself.

The Course and Landowners

The land on which the course was built was originally partly arable and devoted largely to the growing of oats, barley and wheat, and partly grazing pastures. On a number of fairways, the gentle undulations caused by many, many years of ploughing to a regular pattern can still be discerned. Similarly, the rough outline of some fields can be traced by reference to the position of those old oak trees that still remain; sadly the elms have gone.

In 1843, the three principal landowners were the Earl of Lovelace, George Banks and William Speer who rented out most of their land in this locality to Isaac Dagwell, Francis Elworthy, George Heath, John Walker and William Wheston. At that time the whole of the area subsequently covered by the course lay within the parishes of Thames Ditton, Long Ditton and Claygate: Claygate became a parish in its own right in 1840, but prior to that time it was part of the parish of Thames Ditton.

From old maps dating from the latter part of the nineteenth century, it would appear that the original nine-hole course lay mainly to the east of The Waffrons's farmhouse. As The Waffrons is not indicated on the Tithe Map of 1843, it was built presumably sometime after 1843; I have not been able to trace the derivation of its name.

It would also seem that sometime after 1843, the Earl of Lovelace acquired any land on which the course was built that may have been owned previously by either the Banks and/or Speer families, and that the Ritchie family were tenants of The Waffrons for a period when A. H. Lisner was the lessee.

With the commencement of work on extending the course to 18 holes in the autumn of 1896, some additional land was utilised to the south, down towards Claygate's Red Lane, and to the west of The Waffrons, towards Telegraph Hill. The latter was so-called from the Admiralty Semaphore Telegraph station built on it in 1822. This was one of a chain of semaphore stations stretching from The Admiralty in Whitehall to Portsmouth. This system of communication operated until 1847 when these stations were closed down forever, following the invention and success of the electric telegraph. The second nine holes were opened for play on 13th March, 1897.

More about the course will be revealed in subsequent chapters.

The Establishment of Golf in Surrey

Surrey is reputed to be the cradle of English golf. The first regularly organised golf club in the county, apart from the Royal Blackheath Club which was founded in 1608, was the London Scottish at Wimbledon which dates from 1865. Then followed Clapham G.C. in 1872. For the most part the golfers of those early years were exiled Scots who had elected to come on a civilizing mission southwards, who had brought their national game with them, and who had chosen with magnanimous disinterestedness, to bear the self-imposed burden of teaching their English brethren the game - or so said A. J. Robertson in 1905. It would seem that some of the Club's present Scottish members still feel much the same as Robertson did 80 years ago!

During the next thirty years a further 36 clubs were founded in Surrey. These included Tooting Bec (1888), Epsom (1889), Thames Ditton and Esher (1891), Richmond (1891), Mid-Surrey (1892), Prince's at Mitcham (1892), Woking (1893), Claygate (1895), Home Park (1895), New Zealand at Byfleet (1895), and, of course, Surbiton (1895).

These early golfers had their problems as many of these courses were established on commons. This was true of Thames Ditton and Esher, also of Claygate, but not as it happened of Surbiton. The general public in England regarded the game as a strange and weird importation. It was not in the least understood, and as a general rule the public were frankly hostile to it. It was considered to be the correct thing to 'field' the ball. Obliging mothers of hopeful sons would invite their boys to pick up the ball lying on the putting surface and run back with it 150 yards to the player who, for a moment, had congratulated himself that a splendid shot from a difficult lie had met its reward. Family cricket pitches were set up on the best kept putting greens, wilfully deaf ears were turned to warning cries of 'Fore'. There were always contumacious members of the public to ferment a real or fancied grievance about the sacrifices which were being extracted from the people in order to minister to the privileged amusement of a small band of golfers. The golfer's lot in Surrey was not an easy one in those days.

We still have some similar problems today. I recall that when playing with Tommy Weston in November 1985, he struck a good, straight tee shot on the eighteenth which landed on the fairway near to the bell, only to discover on breasting the rise that some small boys had 'fielded' his ball for keeps. Alas this fine old ship's bell from the M.V. 'Ulster Monarch', which was presented to the Club in 1950 by Harry Denny in his year of Captaincy, was stolen by persons unknown around this time. The bell near the twelfth green was also stolen at the same time.

Whilst on the subject of the eighteenth and its bell, before the last war there used to be a tall, wooden periscope by the tee to enable players to see if the fairway beyond the rise was clear. Mrs. Madge Picknett recalls an occasion when on peering through it she found two great eyes staring back at her. An owl had fallen in the periscope, which was by that time in a state of disrepair. Needless to say she rescued the owl which flew off apparently none the worse for its experience.

I appear to have digressed somewhat from the theme of this chapter: let me revert to certain events in 1896 and 1897.

The Spring Meeting of 1896

As already stated, this was the Club's first Spring Meeting. It was held over two days, Thursday 14th and Saturday 16th May. On the first day the results of the principal competition, for which the first prize was a set of golf clubs, were:

A. B. Tomkins	99–22 = 77	F. B. Norris	108–18 = 90
G. T. Wrench	113–26 = 87	W. E. James	121–30 = 91
W. Ford-Lewis	110–22 = 88	C. A. Hewitt	117–25 = 92
A. C. Fairbairn	120–30 = 90	H. Wood-Smith	117–16 = 101

On Saturday the prize was a gold medal and the results were:

A. Nisbet	92–16 = 76	W. Ford-Lewis	117–22 = 95
T. Gourlay	113–24 = 89	S. Ellson	117–22 = 95
F. B. Norris	107–18 = 89	E. Hall	125–28 = 97
A. Mays-Smith	101–12 = 89	P. L. Foxwell	123–26 = 97
A. B. Tomkins	105–15 = 90	J. W. Dickinson	123–24 = 99
D. F. Thompson	115–24 = 91	R. Mould	133–30 = 103
W. E. James	124–30 = 94	A. C. Fairbairn	175–35 = 140

These scores reveal several interesting aspects of the game in those days. Firstly, with the clubs and balls then available, not helped most probably by the conditions of the greens and fairways, breaking 90 (gross) was obviously quite an achievement for any amateur golfer. Secondly, there appeared to be no limit to one's handicap. Thirdly, Tomkins had his handicap cut by seven strokes after winning by 10 strokes on the Thursday. Lastly, golfers had no inhibitions about returning very high scores – who in this day and age would dare return a Medal card of 175 for 18 holes!

You have to admire our predecessors, or would they all have returned much lower scores with our modern equipment, more suitable clothing and better balls and course? Even so, Ian Woosnam, who played at Surbiton in 1986, had a 16 on one hole in a proper competition (not at Surbiton) in 1985, while the highest recorded score by a decent golfer was in the Shawnee Invitation (Pennsylvania) for women in 1912 when one competitor took 166 strokes at the short 16th. Her tee shot landed in water and the ball floated down river but, with her husband at the oars, they took to the water and caught up with her ball one and a half miles downstream. When back on dry land, the only way back to the green was through a wood. It makes one think that some of our own misfortunes are, in retrospect, not so bad after all – there but for the Grace of God go I!

The Spring Meeting and AGM of 1897

It is fitting to conclude this chapter with a mention of these two events as they relate to, and mark the time, when the course was extended to 18 holes with a total playing length of 4,541 yards.

The Spring Meeting was held, as was then the custom, over two days – Thursday 8th and Saturday 10th April, 1897. Thursday's competition was a ladies' and gentlemen's foursomes, which was won by Miss Koe and E. S. Pipkin with a score of 117–17 = 100; runners up were Mrs. Forsell and E. S. Trouncer (126–15 = 111) and Mr. and Mrs. R. Mould (136–19 = 117). Concurrently, the ladies' singles prize was won by Miss May Hobson (136–24 = 112), with Mrs. Mould (141–21 = 120) as runner up, and the gentlemen's singles by A. S. Mays-Smith (88–9 = 79), with C. F. Nesham (107–26 = 81) as runner-up.

The competition on Saturday took the form of a Medal, the results of which were:

A. S. Mays-Smith	94–9 = 85	A. Nisbet	100–8 = 92
E. Hall	113–28 = 85	C. A. Hewitt	117–25 = 92
P. Waterlow	101–15 = 86	A. B. Tomkins	104–9 = 95
P. L. Foxwell	112–26 = 86	H. E. Walton	115–20 = 95
S. N. Corlett	99–11 = 88	C. F. Nesham	122–26 = 96
R. H. Lafage	119–30 = 89	R. Popkiss	116–18 = 98
H. A. Perkin	106–15 = 91		

Mays-Smith won the tie on the play-off, also the aggregate prize for the Spring meeting with a net 164 (79 + 85).

These excitements were followed, on the Saturday evening, by the Club's AGM with the Captain, Bulmer Howell, in the chair. He referred to the opening of the second nine holes, and remarked that:

> '. . . *every member who had mentioned the subject to him had expressed delight with the addition. They were greatly indebted to Mr. Lisner for the work he had done, not only on the new but also on the original nine holes. The old course of nine holes has been effectively drained during the winter.*'

In reply, Lisner thanked the Chairman for his complimentary remarks and the company for the kind way in which they received them. He stated that he would continue to make improvements till the course was as perfect as labour and money could make it.

So by 1897 the Club, now called Surbiton, was really on its way with an 18 hole course, a clubhouse, regular competitions, and a membership of about 130. It was then a rather exclusive Club with probably more attention being paid to applicants' social standing than to their playing ability, although the membership included some very good golfers. How the Club was financed during these early years is not entirely clear. Obviously, there was an income from members' subscriptions, green fees and the like, but these were fairly modest and it would seem that the main financial burden was carried by Lisner personally who one suspects was a rather wealthy gentleman and a keen golfer. Somewhat surprisingly, Lisner does not appear in any of the above listings of competitors. Perhaps he was an indifferent player, or maybe competitions were not to his taste and that he preferred to direct his energies to 'running' the Club behind the scenes. During these initial years his name appears variously as secretary, treasurer and committee member, sometimes all three at the same time: we can be virtually certain that the Club owes its very existence to the energies, enthusiasm and financial support provided by this one gentleman. While others undoubtedly contributed in their various ways, and without the active interest of members there is no club, it is Mr. A. H. Lisner, gentleman of Pall Mall, who we should regard as the Club's founder. Thank you sir for the considerable pleasure you have given to many hundreds of people over the years, we all owe you a deep debt of gratitude.

CHAPTER 2

LEASES PRIOR TO 1957

The earliest lease I have been able to uncover is that of 1906. Prior to this lease I assume that the land was leased to A. H. Lisner by the Earl of Lovelace and that Lisner under-leased it to Surbiton Golf Club. Presumably Lisner's lease expired in 1906 or thereabouts, but this is all conjecture in the absence of documentary evidence to the contrary.

The Lease of 1906

On the 30th November, 1906, The Right Honorable Mary Caroline, Dowager Countess of Lovelace (the lessor), granted Richard Mould Esquire of the Fairmile, Cobham; Aubrey Flory Howard, Merchant of 138 Leadenhall Street, London; John Henry Harrison-Hogge of Stanshope, Foley Road, Claygate and Charles Augustus Hewitt, an Underwriter at Lloyds, all acting on behalf of Surbiton Golf Club, a 21-year lease on 137 acres, 1 rood and 4 perches of land, including The Waffrons, lying mainly in the parish of Thames Ditton and partly in the parish of Long Ditton. The land comprised about 127 acres of pasture, 3 acres of woodland, and some 6 acres of The Waffrons including the farmhouse and its cottages, gardens and orchard.

The yearly rent for this lease was £300 payable in equal quarterly instalments, and was subject to six months' notice of termination in the fourteenth year. There were many conditions. These included, for example, an additional rent of £25 per annum for every acre that the lessees ploughed, dug or broke up without the lessor's prior permission. Similar penalties applied to the cutting down, lopping or ripping out of any trees or shrubs. The lessees were not permitted to cut down any hedges, coppices or underwood until they had achieved seven year's full growth, nor suffer the same to stand longer than ten years without being cut, but only after giving the lessor appropriate notice.

There were three other restrictive clauses of particular interest. The lessees were permitted, but not obliged, to erect a clubhouse, subject to the plans of it being approved by the lessor, provided that the building was of no lesser value than £1,500. And if the lessees decided to erect such a clubhouse, they were then required to paint the inside '*. . . with three coats of good oil and white lead paint in a proper and workmanlike manner, and will paper, varnish, colour and whitewash such parts thereof as shall or ought to be papered, varnished, coloured and whitewashed*'. The same applied to the outside, but this had to be done every three years. If this wasn't enough, the lessor would pay the lessees £650 if she terminated the lease after fourteen years, or not more than £500 if the lessees terminated the lease after the same period.

Secondly, the lessees were not allowed, without prior permission, to '... *destroy or in anyway damage the greens, approaches, bunkers and grounds of the said golf course, but will maintain it in all respects in good order and condition during the term of the lease*'. This and related provisions may appear, at first sight, to be entirely reasonable, but knowing the habit of Greens Committees to alter courses and their hazards, it must have been rather irksome to have had to seek permission every time some new inspiration struck them.

Thirdly, The Waffrons at that time was occupied by Mrs. Fanny Ritchie, widow, and under the terms of the lease the Club was effectively obliged to underlease it to her and to maintain the property in '... *good and tenantable repair and condition, damage by fire excepted, at the Club's own expense*'. Moreover, the Club could not assign or underlet The Waffrons without the previous consent of the lessor, although such consent would not be unreasonably withheld in the case of a '*respectable and responsible tenant*'.

These examples of the conditions of the lease very much favoured the lessor as observed by the lessor's solicitors who commented to their client that, '... *the lease is an extremely beneficial one from the point of view of the rental, representing as it does a considerable increase in income*'.

As was customary in those days, much of the lease was concerned with maintaining the land in good order for future generations. But the lessor's advisers were not without an eye for possible gain in that '... *subject to it not causing any serious interference with the said golf course, it should be lawful for the lessor at any time upon giving one month's notice to resume possession of such parts of the demised premises as may be required for the purposes of a railway or for building purposes*'. How one could build a railway without seriously interfering with the golf course is rather beyond me!

Leases of 1919, 1924 and 1932

The lease of 1906 did not in fact last its full term. It was superseded by new leases in 1919 and 1924, and these in turn by the 21-year lease of 1932, which, with some supplementary agreements, lasted its full 21 years, even though ownership of the land in question passed from the Lovelace family to others in 1937.

The lease of the 24th June, 1932, contained many clauses which were similar to the lease of 1906. Surprisingly, the yearly rent remained unchanged at £300. The Trustees that signed the lease on behalf of the Club were Eustace Sherrard, Sidney Archbutt, Guarnerius Withers, James Hossack, Samuel Dyas and John Grant. There was the usual protection for the tenant of The Waffrons, then Cyril Coggan.

A map included with the 1932 lease probably explains the reason why new leases were drawn up in 1919 and 1924, as the configuration of the land had changed, especially with the building of the Kingston By-Pass. Prior to that event, the fifth hole, which at over 600 yards (par 6) was said to be the longest in England, extended to the far side of where the By-Pass now stands.

From this map the reader can ascertain largely for himself the overall configuration of the course as it was in the 1930s. Apart from the length of the 5th, note also that most of what are now the 15th, 16th and 18th holes were not then part of the course, while to the east the course extended down to Woodstock Lane.

The Agreement of 1937

At the risk of already having bored some readers, let me conclude this chapter with mention of the Supplemental Agreement of 7th July, 1937. This Agreement is important if only because it more or less set the final shape of the course, not quite, but nearly so for all practical purposes.

In this Agreement, the lessor, Harry Gillitt, and the Club's Trustees who were still Sherrard, Archbutt, Withers, Hossack, Dyas and Grant, agreed to an exchange of land. It was then that the present 15th, 16th and 18th holes took shape. In exchange for this additional land, the 5th was shortened by some 11 acres and the eastern part of the course beyond the present visitors' car park down to Woodstock Lane was given up by the Club. With a small gain overall in favour of the lessor, the annual rent was reduced from £300 to £297.

On the land given up on the 5th, which shortened this hole from 577 yards (the green was then just this side of the By-Pass) to its present 395 yards, was built a printing works for the Ordnance Survey when their works at Southampton were badly damaged by bombing during the last war. Around that time, Major-General Geoffrey Cheetham, C.B., D.S.O., M.C., who was head of the Ordnance Survey, became the tenant of The Waffrons, the previous tenant being Sir Donald Simpson, and he and his wife joined the Club.

Before describing the traumas of the 1950s when the 1932 lease expired, let us first reminisce about some of the events that affected the Club during the last war.

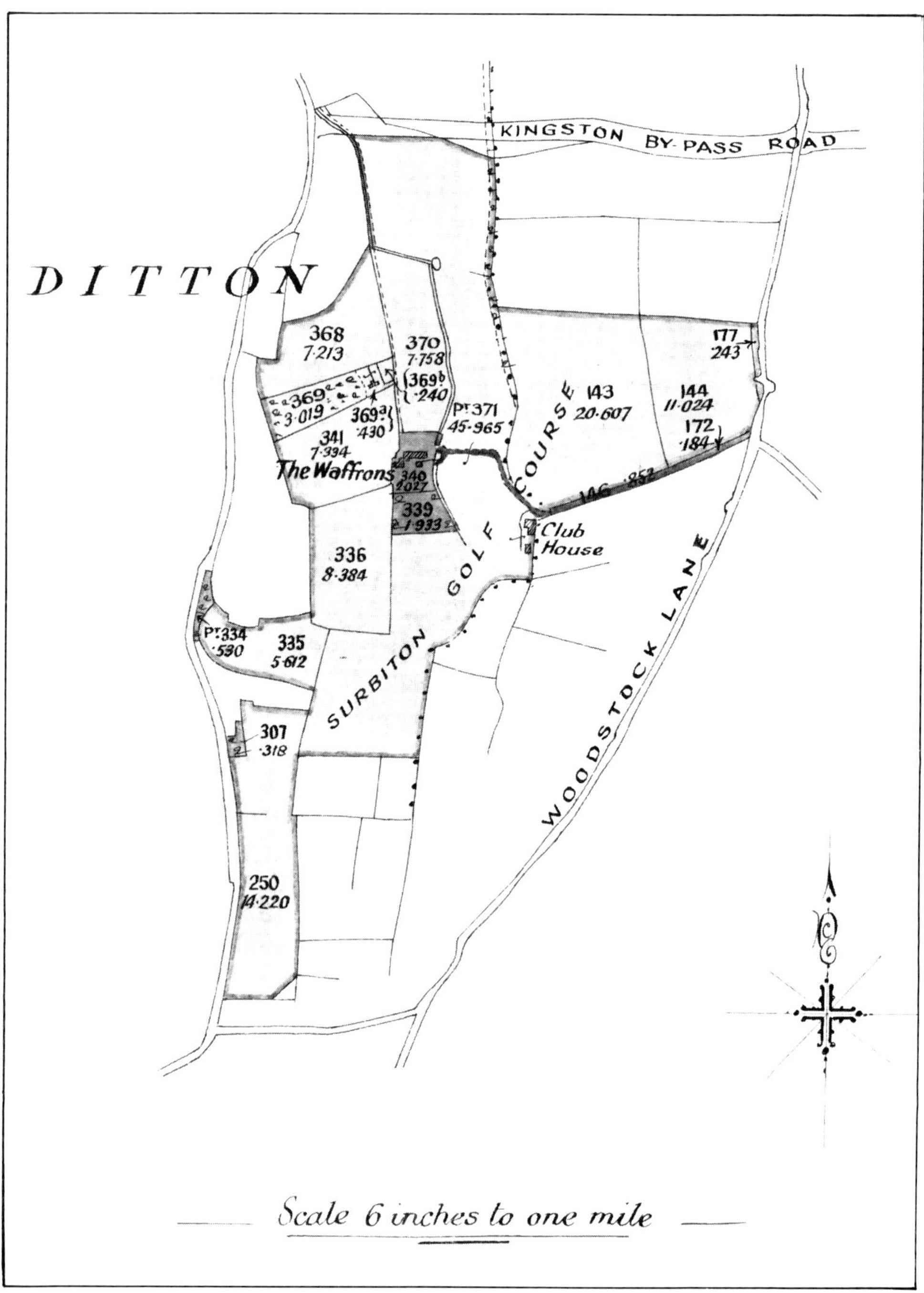

Surbiton Golf Club 1932

CHAPTER 3

SOME WARTIME RECOLLECTIONS

One of the Club's contributions to the war effort – the Second World War that is, as there are no records of what happened to the Club and its members in the 1914–18 war – was its loss of six and a bit holes. These were the 5th, 6th, 7th, and part of the 8th up to the road, and the 14th, 15th and 16th which were ploughed up in the early days of the war for the growing of cereals and potatoes. According to Bill Farenden and others, after these holes were ploughed up a round consisted of starting from the ninth and playing through to the thirteenth, followed by the seventeenth and eighteenth, the first to the fourth, and ended up by repeating the first seven of these holes to make up the necessary eighteen.

Much more serious and important than the loss of six holes was, of course, the sacrifice of those Club members who laid down their lives during the war. Undoubtedly, there must have been some, but alas the names of all those who made this supreme 'contribution' are not recorded, and thus perforce these wartime recollections are confined to more mundane matters.

Reverting to Bill Farenden's recollections, he took up golf in 1940 as a consequence of the invitation the Club extended to the local Chief Air Raid Warden: this was that any members of the Civil Defence were welcome to play at Surbiton for one shilling per round. Bill being a warden, and having recently acquired a set of second-hand clubs, took advantage of this generous offer and cycled up in the evenings whenever possible; double summer time was a blessing in this regard. Bill got to learn and love the game and became a full member in 1943, and at 92 years of age rightly enjoys the privilege of being one of the Club's few Honorary Members.

Madge Picknett, another Honorary Member, and her husband, joined the Club in 1937. Sidney Picknett, with a 9 handicap, was played in by three Committee Members. He drove the 12th in two to land his second shot midst the Captain and his partners playing ahead of him, and was duly elected! To move on in time, Mrs. Picknett recalls that during the war the fairways of those holes that were still playable were narrowed, calling for accurate hitting and resulting in many lost balls. These became very scarce and, when found later, were handed to the pro, Jim Coleman, who repainted them for resale to the members.

Later, sheep were grazed over part of the course. The water retentive nature of the soil caused the sheep to develop foot rot to the point where they had, believe it or not, to be fitted out with little rubber boots. Mrs. Picknett recalls that some of the lambs had to be hand-reared in the Club's kitchen, and remembers one lamb which thought he was a dog and guarded the premises. He charged at her on a number of occasions when she cycled up the path from Hinchley Wood, with the result that she had to be rescued by other members from this angry wee beastie! Mrs. Picknett and Walter Bradley also remember that a number of 10 foot poles were erected across certain fairways to deter landings by enemy aircraft and gliders. These were hit so frequently by golf balls that the poles were removed and replaced by grassed ridges some 6 or 7 feet in height. The remains of two of these ridges can be found on the second and third fairways; they were reduced to their present size after the war at the request of many members who were unable to carry them at their original height – some of us find it difficult to carry them even now!

'Pip' Whitehorn's recollections, another Honorary Member who joined the Club in 1935 and was, as far as is known, the Club's longest serving member until sadly he died in January 1987, confirm much of the foregoing. And he, like some other members, recounts the partial destruction by a bomb of two old cottages, the Waffrons Cottages, located to the right of the eleventh tee. These cottages were subsequently destroyed later in the war by a flying bomb, colloquially known in those days as a Doodlebug, and as a result of this they had to be demolished for safety reasons. Fortunately, no-one was hurt when the cottages were bombed, nor were there any casualties to any members or staff on or about the course during the war from other enemy actions. Oddly enough, the Virginia creeper that used to clamber over these cottages survived the bombs and still flourishes today on some nearby trees.

Almost every member of every vintage will know that the tree-fringed crater to the left of the ninth fairway was caused by a wartime bomb, or landmine, but it is less widely known that there was another bomb crater farther up the hill to the left of the eighteenth fairway. This was caused by a large bomb, and Mr. Whitehorn and some others recall that it was hand-filled by club members, although the scars of it are still visible today. As one might expect, these bombs blew out the windows of the clubhouse and caused some other minor damage to it.

Not all the damage to the course was caused by the enemy. The area now occupied by the sixteenth green was used as a bombing range by the Welsh Guards who were stationed at Sandown Park Racecourse. In 1985, over forty years later, a live hand-grenade was found by the ground staff in this area, a fairly common occurrence in earlier post-war years.

The fact that the Club managed to survive the war, and to remain open for play, was quite an achievement and reflects credit on the Captains of the Club during this period, Messrs. Inglis, Maclean, Mason, Hindson, Shields and Davie, also Capt. C. E. Crowne, who was Secretary for the best part of twenty years, Jim Coleman the pro, the Steward and his wife, Frank and Chris Frend, and not least of all those members and wartime guests who kept playing and assisted the Club in all manner of ways.

In early 1940 the part-time volunteer force known as the Local Defence Volunteers was created, renamed the Home Guard in the following year. A keen member of the Club, Mr. Maidment, rallied around him some 40 members and formed what was to become known as the Golf Club Platoon of the local Home Guard Company. It set up its headquarters in the billiard room of The Waffrons, though a lot of time was spent in the clubhouse where the arms and ammunition were stored. The Platoon spent many hours training, with some assistance from the Welsh Guards, and carried out nightly guard duties. Its officers were Bertie Blunt, Platoon Commander, and Fred Walters, Platoon Officer, while Charles Walker was Sergeant and Walter Bradley the Platoon Corporal.

Shortly before the Home Guard was disbanded in December 1944, a new Platoon came onto the course and made their HQ in a dugout in the woods at the side of the 7th tee.

During the war, Peter Holford, while he was awaiting call up, and the son of William Ross, decided to see how many rounds they could play during one day. So one morning, after all-night Home Guard duty and a light breakfast, they set off on their bicycles and accomplished six rounds (108 holes), probably a Club record.

Both Tim Pyrke and Walter Bradley recall that women prisoners from Holloway were used for potato picking in the fields adjoining the 18th and in the fields that the 6th and 7th holes had then become. When working near the 18th, they often hurled abuse and obscenities at passing lady members. On one occasion, two of the prisoners escaped through the woods bordering the 7th.

Several men members have expressed to me their gratitude for the way the lady members managed to conjure out of their meagre wartime rations tasty light refreshments for Club members on appropriate occasions. Such contributions to the wellbeing of the Club during these very difficult times should not go unrecorded – a belated thank you ladies.

While not particularly associated with the war years, but just as much with the years before and immediately after the war, mention should be made of the wildlife that several members observed around this period – if nothing else, it is a pleasant way to end this chapter which dwells on times we all hope will never be repeated.

There is, of course, still a lot of wildlife to be seen around the course, but less varied now than would appear to be the case in earlier years. I have been told of frequent sightings of foxes, rabbits, stoats, snakes, squirrels, hedgehogs, even the occasional badger, and the activities of moles, if not the moles themselves. There was also a great variety of birds including sparrowhawks, all sorts of woodpeckers, jays, and a rookery close to the 7th hole, as well as the more common bird life that is always with us. Of course, quite a few of these species are still about, indeed last winter a fox ran a few feet in front of me as I was about to tee off on the 17th, but in general the wildlife today tends to be less obvious.

The Ladies' Section 1951
The Ladies' Captain, Mrs. Tess Hurlock, the third from the left, front row

Recent Captains of the Ladies' Section, from left to right, Mrs. E. Kinnock (1983), Mrs. F. Pretsell (1982), Mrs. E. Ramage (1986), Mrs. J. Buckland (1984) and Mrs. Z. Gee (1985)

CHAPTER 4

1957 – A YEAR FOR CELEBRATION

1957 was undoubtedly the Club's most traumatic year since its founding, although both 1939 and 1952 ran it a fairly close second; but first let us go back some years in order to set the scene.

The Lovelace Lease

On the 27th June, 1932, The Right Honourable Mary Caroline, Dowager Countess of Lovelace, granted a second lease of 21 years to the Club for an annual rent of £300 on similar terms to her lease of 1906 which was described in chapter 2. The land then comprised 135 acres, 2 roods and 21 perches and covered very much the same area as the lease of 1906, although it now stopped short at the Kingston By-Pass and embraced what has since become the Old Wandsworthians' sports ground. Moreover, it did not include what are now the eastern halves of the 16th and 18th holes, nor the strip of woodland between the 13th hole and 14th tee known as Smith's Hill. But as with the previous lease, it did include The Waffrons which the Club sub-let (at that time) to Cyril Coggan for an annual rent of £200.

In early 1937, Mary, Countess of Lovelace, who died in 1941, sold that part of her estate on which the course stands to Henry Gillitt of Coventry who then became owner in fee simple of the Club. And shortly before the last war Gillitt agreed to exchange the Old Wandsworthians' sports field and land beyond the present 5th green down to the Kingston By-Pass, for land which is now the 18th and part of the ground on which the present 16th and 17th holes now stand. For this exchange Gillitt paid the Club £5,000, part of which was to compensate the farmer for the loss of his land (the 16th and 18th), and part for the building of new fences. More worrying at this time was the proposal to build a public thoroughfare across the course from the clubhouse to Old Claygate Lane which would have facilitated, inter alia, extending the housing in Claygate Lane, Hinchley Wood, around Telegraph Hill. The war put paid to this idea, if it ever was a serious plan. The annual rent after this exchange was marginally reduced to £297.

Immediately after the war, Gillitt, together with his partners and co-owners John Heritage-Peters of Coventry and Nathan Davis of London, concluded a deed with the Club's new Trustees, but this did not affect the second Lovelace lease of 1932, i.e. the Club's lease would still expire on 24th June, 1953.

The By-Pass Threat

While the above events were taking place, a real threat to the Club's future arose. This was the announcement in 1935 that the Ministry of Transport and Surrey County Council were considering building a new major road to relieve traffic congestion through Esher. Part of this road, i.e. from where it would branch off from the Kingston By-Pass (A3), was planned to go through several holes of the course. The result of the Public Inquiry held in April 1939 was never formally published due to the outbreak of war. So this threat was averted, by Hitler if you like.

The idea of an Esher By-Pass was revived in 1959, but by then several different routes were proposed, none of which posed a serious threat to the Club. In any event, the land in question had been rezoned in 1946 from building development to agricultural land, later to become part of the Green Belt, although this would not necessarily have prevented a really determined governmental authority from pressing ahead if it had so wished. The full story of the Esher By-Pass is well documented and does not require repetition here.

With these worries out of the way, let us return to 1952, the year before the Club's lease was due to expire.

Up for Auction

On the 22nd October, 1952, the lessors put the golf course and The Waffrons up for auction as two separate lots at the London Auction Market. The course, including the clubhouse, car park and all buildings, comprised some 133 acres with an official course length of 5,976 yards. Vacant possession was offered from 25th June, 1953. Before the auction took place, the Club approached both Surbiton Council and Esher Council in the hope that they would consider purchasing the course. In the event, neither council felt they could commit up to perhaps £30,000 of ratepayers' money to acquire the course. At the auction itself the highest bid received was £19,500. As this was below the undisclosed reserve price, the property was withdrawn and remained on the market for sale. Further approaches by the Club to the councils concerned to purchase the course were again unsuccessful. The Club's future after June 1953 was unknown.

June 1953 came and went and with its passing the landlords permitted the Club to continue using the course and clubhouse under a rental agreement of indeterminate duration, and with no guarantee of future occupancy, at a rent of £870 per annum. This insecurity of tenure, as it became general knowledge, made it difficult to retain staff and a number of members started drifting away to join other clubs. Attempts by the Club to arrive at some sounder basis of occupancy and/or to acquire the freehold, but at what price and with what funds are not recorded, were unsuccessful.

For Sale Again and Sold

The next shock came when the Club was notified that the course, The Waffrons, and some surrounding farmland, were to be put up for public auction for the second time on 19th February, 1957. Shortly before this auction, the Club was advised that the course would be offered for sale in four separate lots. Unless all four lots were purchased the Club looked to be doomed.

Before the auction took place, a Special General Meeting of all classes of members was held on 12th January - more about this in a moment. Suffice it to say at this point that this meeting did not give the Club's officials authority to make a bid at the auction, nor did they have the funds to do so in any event, although the ultimate objective of purchasing the course was decided at this meeting as we shall see.

The auction was attended by Freddie Pyrke, Walter Bradley and Ernest Newman, but just before the proceedings commenced, those present were informed that the lots of interest to the Club, together with the adjoining Manor Farm, had been sold by private treaty to Mr. Laurence Knight of Hanover Square, London, who was related to, but not a member of, the firm, Knight, Frank and Ruttley.

Immediately after the auction the Club's representatives contacted Mr. Knight who offered to give the Club a lease until March 1958: this was obviously unacceptable. Subsequent contacts with the new owner led in due course to an ultimatum: it was that if the Club wished to purchase the course and its buildings, he (Knight) was prepared to sell the freehold for £26,000, excluding the practice ground which he intended to retain as part of Manor Farm, but he would throw in as part of the deal a ten acre field at the end of the first hole. From this it will be gathered that the practice ground in question was on the far side of the present members' car park and extended alongside the eighteenth fairway to the top of the hill. The loss of a proper practice ground was a blow, and continues to be much missed today, but the need to find £26,000, subsequently reduced to £25,000, was a far greater problem and challenge.

While this amount of money may seem relatively modest by present-day standards, it was not an inconsiderable sum in the mid 1950s. For the financial year ending 31st March, 1956, the Club's total income was £6,411 and expenditure £6,305; accumulated funds amounted to £427. Membership fees for full men members, of which there were 186, at 15 guineas per annum were hardly a significant source of income in relation to the sum of money involved; there were no entrance fees at that time, and income from visiting societies was not then a feature of the golfing scene.

The Way Ahead

Three Special General Meetings of all classes of members – full and five day members, ladies, juveniles, honorary and non-playing members, the lot – were held on 12th January, 16th March and 6th April, 1957. At the first of these meetings, the Captain, Freddie Pyrke, outlined the problems the Club were facing and sought members' views on possible solutions. It was not until Mrs. Gwendoline Betts, a former Captain of the Ladies' Section (1934 and 1935) whose father and mother had both been Captains in their time, and who had been a Chairman of The Urban District Council of Esher, suggested that the Club should endeavour to purchase the freehold and then think about how to raise the money, that the way ahead suddenly became much clearer. The Committee was then given the full backing of members in its efforts to find ways and means to purchase the freehold, and the Note scheme, first mooted in 1952, was agreed as being the most suitable fund-raising mechanism, details of which had already been circulated to members on 31st December, 1956.

The second meeting of 16th March was the most crucial when the Captain told the members that unless Mr. Knight's final offer of £25,000 was accepted by 18th March, he would consider himself free to dispose of the land elsewhere as he so wished. The Captain informed the meeting that in response to the Committee's appeal, i.e. the Note scheme, a total of £12,363 had been offered by members, and that despite efforts to obtain more permanent forms of finance from other quarters, the Committee had only been able to secure temporary finance from the Club's bankers. He had offered Mr. Knight £23,000 that morning, but the owner had rejected this and, therefore, unless the full amount of £25,000 could be paid, members would have no alternative but to pass a resolution winding up the Club. After considerable discussion, and some counter suggestions and proposals, the meeting finally voted and passed Mrs. Betts's proposal, seconded by Reg Bullen, that the offer of £25,000 be accepted, subject to contract.

At the third meeting on 6th April, the Captain stated that the amount subscribed by members had now reached £14,610 in the form of 'A' Notes and £1,220 in the form of Debentures; he thanked the subscribers for their fine response. He then informed the meeting that the Eagle Star Insurance Company was prepared to advance money on certain terms, which included the giving of personal guarantees by some members. It was therefore proposed to cancel the issue of Debentures and to give members who had subscribed to them the opportunity of either purchasing 'A' or 'B' Notes, or having their money refunded. The following two resolutions were put to the meeting and carried unanimously:

'1. That the finance of the Golf Course proceed on the approximate basis of £15,000 or £16,000 of members' 'A' and 'B' Notes and the insurance company's mortgage of £5,000 or £4,000 and that the purchase scheme be amended by deleting reference to Debentures.

2. That the sub-committee dealing with the purchase be given full discretionary powers to enable them to deal in the most equitable manner they deem necessary with subscribers and their contributions'.

Thanks were also expressed to William Dewe, a councillor representing the Hinchley Wood ward of Esher Urban District Council, who for his own account undertook to purchase The Waffrons for £5,800, and without whose help the purchase of the Club would not have been possible. Again with the benefit of hindsight the loss of The Waffrons, like that of the practice ground, was a pity; one can only imagine today what a splendid clubhouse The Waffrons would have made. In all fairness there was no alternative at that time, and Mr. Dewe was not exactly acquiring a property in first-class condition. The Waffrons had been empty for several years and had been severely vandalised since its last tenant, Maj.-Gen. Geoffrey Cheetham, C.B., D.S.O., M.C., departed a few years beforehand.

Purchase Completed

Contracts for the purchase of the course, its buildings and The Waffrons were exchanged on 11th April, 1957. The price was £25,000, less £5,800 for the resale of The Waffrons to Dewe. Surbiton Golf Club Limited, a company limited by guarantee having no share capital, was formed in May 1957 which then granted a 21-year lease to the Club. At long last, after many years of doubt and insecurity, the Club's tenure was secured. As a matter of interest, £25,000 in 1957 is approximately equivalent to £210,000 in today's (1986) money.

'A' Notes

A few words concerning the above-mentioned 'A' Notes are necessary. This was a scheme devised largely by Duncan Smith whereby the purchase of Notes would give the members concerned a subscription relief in lieu of interest on the monies loaned to the Club. These Notes had a face value of £10 each and would be repurchased at that price by the Club 'as and when funds became available' – a slim prospect in the eyes of many members in 1957. No member was permitted to subscribe for more than 30. Registered holders of 'A' Notes in the books of Surbiton Golf Club Limited were, and still are, entitled to annual subscription relief corresponding to their class of membership. In the case of full men members this is for each Note one-thirtieth, for full lady members one-twentieth, and so on pro-rata for other membership classes. In retrospect this has obviously been a good investment for long-serving members, but in 1957 it was a much more speculative proposition. For many individuals putting down up to £300 of their own money at a time when the annual subscription was less than £16 must have seemed a long term, each-way bet at best; the rate of inflation was low, and the wages and cost of living explosion of the second half of the 1960s and 1970s was not then perceived or expected. Again to put matters into perspective, £300 in 1957 is equivalent to about £2,500 today. Safeguards were also necessary in the event of subscribers leaving the Club or falling on hard times. Over the years the Club's Trustees have repurchased an increasing number of 'A' Notes at market prices for conversion into 'B' Notes (with no subscription relief) as they have become available. While some newer members may mutter from time to time about the benefits that the remaining 'A' Note Holders still enjoy, it should be remembered that without their financial support and the risks they took in 1957, the Club would most probably not exist today.

For the record, a list of 'A' Note Holders as at July 1957 is given in the Appendix to this chapter. From a balance sheet drawn up on 8th August, 1957, it appears that 1,522 'A' Notes and 78 'B' Notes each of £10 were taken up by that date representing a total of £16,000.

The Role of the Trustees

As mention has been made of the Trustees, it is perhaps appropriate to comment at this point that Trustees have been appointed by the Club's Committee for very many years to act for and on behalf of the Club, and were not an innovation brought about by the 1952 or 1957 crises. As the name implies, the Trustees hold the property and effects of the Club in trust for its members and act on the direction of the Committee. The Trustees have a lien on all Club property to indemnify them in respect of their liability.

Some Concluding Comments

I doubt if the above account gives full justice to the traumas of 1957, and more especially to the very considerable time and effort devoted by many members to saving the Club from extinction, but nevertheless I hope it gives a feel of what happened. While it may seem invidious to name a few among so many, it would be equally unfair not to pay tribute to the leadership, energy and inspiration of Freddie Pyrke (Captain 1955 and 1956, but which of course included the first six months of 1957), and to acknowledge the whole-hearted support he received from the 'Purchase' sub-committee of Sir Sydney Camm, Duncan Smith, Bert Boyles, Tony Hartnell (Treasurer), Ernie Newman (Secretary) and Harry Barber – the Club owes these gentlemen, and others not named, a considerable debt of gratitude. I trust it is now clear why I have dedicated this book to Freddie Pyrke.

Once the purchase of the Club had been secured, membership

started to rise again and improvements to the course and clubhouse were put in hand to the extent that funds permitted; a new breath of air was felt by all. To 'celebrate the occasion', Freddie Pyrke introduced a new competition, the Celebration Cup, a mixed foursomes match play event played under handicap limits of 20 for men and 30 for ladies. And the highlight of the celebratory weekend of 1st and 2nd June, 1957, was a match between Sydney Camm and Dai Rees against Robert Greenish and Jim Coleman.

Duncan Smith, Spring 1949

Postscript

As will be apparent from the foregoing, Surbiton Golf Club is owned by Surbiton Golf Club Limited and not, as some members believe, by the 'A' Note Holders: they are not the shareholders of Surbiton Golf Club Limited which has no shareholders. And as already stated it is the Trustees, appointed by the General Committee, who hold the property of the Club in trust for its members, while the Directors of Surbiton Golf Club Limited manage the affairs of that company.

While the Trustees are the ultimate body empowered to handle the disposition of the Club's property, facilities and effects, they may only do so on the direction or by a resolution of the General Committee. So in the final analysis the 'control' of the Club's property and effects resides in the hands of the General Committee of Surbiton Golf Club, a body related to but separate from Surbiton Golf Club Limited.

What then is the General Committee, and who appoints the members of it? Under the Club's Rules, which can only be amended at Annual or Extraordinary General Meetings of members, the General Committee comprises:

— the Captain, who is Chairman of the Committee;
— the immediate past Captain;
— the Vice-Captain;
— the Honorary Treasurer;
— the Trustees of Surbiton Golf Club Limited;
— nine other elected Club members; and
— not more than five Directors of Surbiton Golf Club Limited.

Of the nine elected Club members, three shall retire each year by rotation but shall be eligible for re-election to serve a second three-year term of office. It is also at these (Annual) General Meetings that the members 'appoint', as distinct from 'elect', the Captain, Vice-Captain and Honorary Treasurer.

The foregoing may seem complicated and cumbersome, but it points up the fact that it is through the process of electing ordinary members to the General Committee by their fellow members, that the destiny of the Club is ultimately determined, especially as Captains, Trustees and the like almost invariably reach these positions by first having served as ordinary elected Committee Members. Far better this procedure than for the Club to be owned by shareholders who by acquisition of other shareholders' shares could, if they were unscrupulous people, strip the Club of its assets for personal gain.

This explanation has been included to enlighten those members who may not be entirely clear as to how the Club is owned and managed.

SURBITON GOLF CLUB LIMITED 'A' NOTE HOLDERS

As at 4th July 1957

Adams, Norman
Alexander, Douglas
Allen, John
Allison, Peter
Allsopp, John
Anderson, Robert
Anderson, Robert J.
Andrew, Henry
Astill, Frank
Balfour, Alfred
Barber, Harry
Barnard, William
Barrie, John
Barton, David
Baugh, Edward
Beale, Donald
Beer, Percy
Bell, Norman
Bennett, Peter
Benson, Edgar
Blackwood, Morrison
Boileau, John
Boyles, Bertram
Bradley, Walter
Brant, Clarence
Brewis, John
Brinded, Alexander
Bryant, Richard
Bullen, Reginald
Camm, Sir Sidney
Cooper, George
Cowie, Andrew
Craig, Alastair
Cullen, Arthur
Church, Jeffrey
Denney, Harry
Devereux, William
Dogherty, Wilfred
Douglass, Joseph
Dunsdon, Charles
Dymond, James
Ellis, Leslie
Gillhespy, Edward
Gray, Peter
Gould, Joseph
Greenhalgh, William
Griffiths, William
Hall, Warden
Hannafin, Dennis
Hartnell, Anthony
Hewson, Stewart
Hillier, Alfred
Hilton, Sidney
Hindson, William
Holford, Sidney
Holt, Ronald
Hopper, Ralph
Howell, William
Howells, Arthur
Howse, John
Hughes, Harold
Hughes, Mervyn
Hughes, Stanley
Hurlock, Charles
Hurst, Norman
Ide, Laurence
Inglis, George
Jimenez, Antonio
Jones, Ernest
Keeler, Peter
Kerrigan, Phillip
Kerrigan, Thomas
Kidd, Eric
Kirby, Francis
Lancaster, Peter
Lester, Joseph
Lewis, Leslie
Lewis, Walter
Lofts, Sidney
Lovegrove, Edwin
Macdonald, Donald
Mackenzie, Alexander
Mackenzie, Malcolm
Mallinson, Gerald
McGinn, Andrew
Menzies, Laurence
Middleton, Edward
Mitchell, William
Moore, Desmond
Moore, Leslie
Munrow, William
Muil, James
Merry, Leslie
Nutt, Frederick
Osborne, John
Pelmear, Andrew
Perrott, Archibald
Picknett, Sidney
Porter, Oliver
Pretsell, James
Pride, Eric
Pyrke, Frederick E.
Pyrke, Frederick J. T.
Reginand, Leon
Roberts, Charles
Ross, Dundonald
Ross, Samuel
Ross, William
Roux, Albert
Sampson, William
Sandberg, Julian
Scott, Cyril
Scott, Sidney
Shearn, Norman
Smith, Duncan
Smith, Dudley
Smith, Maurice
Souray, David
Spurr, John
Tarring, Andrew
Taylor, Harry
Warriner, Thomas
Watson, George
Weeks, Percy
Whitehorn, Percy
Whiteside, Alan

Ezekiel, Victor	Marsh, John	Williams, Cyril
Farenden, William	Martin, Frank	Williamson, Graham
Farmar, Alfred	Martin, John	Williamson, Peter
Farrington, William	McDonald, John	Wilson, Frederick
Furby, Cecil	McDowell, Rowland	Woolway, William
Garrud, John		

Anderson, Kathleen	Hamilton, Muriel	Newman, Eveline
Barnard, May	Hewson, Cecily	Pelmear, Annie
Beer, Freda	Hughes, Mabel	Picknett, Madge
Bennet, Georgina	Hughes, Violet	Porter, Edna
Benson, Elsie	Humphrey, Dorothy	Price, Janie
Betts, Gwendoline	Hurst, Patricia	Pyrke, Emily
Blackwood, Kathleen	Inglis, Jean	Ritchie, Blanche
Bullen, Florence	Jessup, Vera	Ross, Lilian
Camm, Lady Hilda	Lewis, Rosemary	Rosser, Alice
Challis, Lilian	Lovegrove, Hilda	Scott, Diana
Davison, Annette	Marsh, Biddy	Tate, Evelyn
Denney, Lena	Merry, Irene	Taylor, Doris
Dewe, Elizabeth	Middleton, Sybil	Walters, Joyce
Ellis, Doris	Moore, Constance	Whiteside, Constance
Ellis, Winifred	Moore, Lottie	Williams, Mary
Garrud, Phyllis	Muil, Marion	Young, Lily

Most probably the above list is not wholly accurate in that some 'A' Note Holders decided around this time to convert some or all of their 'A' Notes (subscription relief, but no interest payable) to 'B' Notes which had no subscription relief, but paid interest at 6% per annum. Also there may well have been some others who decided to acquire 'A' and/or 'B' Notes after the date indicated. Apologies are due to those whose names may have been omitted for one reason or another, and also to all 'B' Note Holders, whose pledges of monies to the Club were no less important in helping the Club to survive.

Since 1957 more than half of the original Notes have been redeemed by the Club at their market values, while some holders have sold their Notes to other Club members. Thus the above list in no way reflects the current remaining Note Holders.

FREEHOLD

THE WELL-KNOWN

SURBITON GOLF COURSE

SURREY

18 Holes Standard Scratch Score: 70

The Sale of the Golf Course presents an opportunity of great appeal to devotees of the game who would welcome an owning interest in a well-known Course.

Situated on high ground in a most accessible position, easily reached by car or fast electric trains. The Course is only 10 miles from the West End and is almost fronting the well-known Kingston By-pass, bounded on the north by Surbiton, on the east by Hook and Chessington, on the south by Hook and Claygate, and on the west by Hinchley Wood and Claygate.

THE OFFICIAL LENGTH OF THE COURSE IS 5,976 YARDS

With spare land not taken into play the area extends to

SOME 133 ACRES

The amenities of the Course include the

MODERN AND ATTRACTIVE CLUBHOUSE

approached from a Gravel Drive from Woodstock Lane

Comprising a well-planned brick-built structure with red-tiled roof and extensive windows overlooking the Course, containing spacious General Lounge with imposing stone fireplace, parquet block flooring. Opening off is the Ladies' Lounge, Ladies' Locker Room (72 lockers) and Ladies' Toilet. On the other side of the General Lounge is the Smoke Room and Members' Bar fitted with open brick-built fireplace, half-panelled walls and built-in seats. The Card Room adjoins the Lounge and the Secretary's Office is close by.

Beyond is the Gentlemen's Locker Room (279 lockers) and Drying Room with ample lavatory accommodation, Bathroom and Gentlemen's Showers. The Kitchen Quarters, which are of liberal proportions, are conveniently arranged at the rear of the Principal Rooms. Approached from the Domestic Quarters is a Flat with Living Room on the Ground Floor and Two Bedrooms, Bathroom and W.C. on the First Floor.

CENTRAL HEATING IS PROVIDED IN THE MAJORITY OF THE ROOMS

MAIN WATER AND ELECTRICITY ARE CONNECTED

THE OUTBUILDINGS

There are Two Timber Buildings a short distance from the main Clubhouse. One is arranged as a Storehouse and Shop and measures about 23ft. by 22ft., with asbestos-tiled roof and Cycle Shed at the rear; the other is about 16ft. by 39ft., with corrugated-iron roof, and beyond is a smaller Shed suitable for a Garage or Store about 14ft. 6in. by 8ft. 6in.

THE CAR PARK

which is close to the Clubhouse, is cinder covered and prote[illegible] approach road. A few yards away from the Car Park is a [illegible]

Particulars from the auction brochure
by
Hillier, Parker, May & Rowden
in conjunction wth
Nightingale, Page & Bennett
London Auction Market
Wednesday, 22nd October, 1952

Detached Freehold Residence

known as

"THE WAFFRONS"

comprising a delightful Old World Farmhouse-type Residence standing in Gardens and well-wooded ground, entirely surrounded by the Golf Course. The House is brick-built, partly rough-cast, with red-tiled and slated roof.

The accommodation comprises:—

Entrance Hall; spacious Lounge, over 40ft. in length by approx. 15ft. 9in.; Dining Room about 21ft. by 19ft.; Conservatory or Games Room with glazed roof and tiled floor, measuring approx. 20ft. by 23ft. 6in., with ample Domestic Accommodation; Dairy with stone floor, and Cloakroom, W.C., and Bathroom. Above are Six well-proportioned Bedrooms ranging from 8ft. 6in. by 15ft. to 15ft. by 21ft. 6in. There are Two Bathrooms with W.C.s. Main Water and Electricity are connected.

THE OUTBUILDINGS

An extensive and lofty timber-built Barn with tiled roof, about 123ft. in length by about 29ft. 6in., divided into two sections, part subdivided to form Three Stalls, with concrete floor and Three spacious Garages. In addition there is a range of brick Buildings used as Potting Sheds, Store and Pigsties. The House stands in about 4 acres of ground, including small Orchard, Kitchen Garden, Paddock and small Grass Tennis Court. The Golf Course and Residence are held on Lease by the Surbiton Golf Club until June, 1953, at a rental of £297 per annum, and will be offered

WITH VACANT POSSESSION

OF THE WHOLE IN JUNE NEXT

The Property is subject to a small apportioned Tithe Rent Charge.

CHAPTER 5

THE OLD COURSE AND RELATED MATTERS

To refresh the reader's memory, the Club's original course was inspired by A. H. Lisner and created to a design of Tom Dunn in 1895.

Tom Dunn

Tom Dunn was the most prolific course designer of his day. He had a reputation for producing layouts that were inexpensive and serviceable It is generally accepted that Dunn was the first designer of inland courses, as distinct from coastal links courses, although both types of course were known as golf links in earlier times. He is quoted as saying repeatedly '*God meant this site to be a golf course*'. As a designer, he was a firm believer in a cross bunker requiring a carry from the tee, another bunker for the approach shot, and, where appropriate, a third fairway bunker for three-shot, par-5 holes.

Dunn, who was born in 1849 and died in 1902, came from a famous golfing family. His father, Willie, and uncle Jamie were both well-known golf-club and ball makers, as well as being first-class players. They achieved fame in a number of celebrated challenge matches against top pros of their day with wagers as high as £400. Tom's first appointment was as professional to Royal Wimbledon in 1870, where he remained for eleven years before moving to North Berwick (1881), and then to Tooting Bec G.C. in 1889. He married Isabel Gourlay of whom it is said '*she was the greatest woman golfer of her day*'. Dunn himself was a first-rate player and teacher, but his many other activities, including course designing and writing, gave him little opportunity to play regularly in professional matches and tournaments. His upbringing and education were far ahead of those of the average club-maker or professional.

During his time, Dunn designed 137 courses in Great Britain, two in France and one in the Canary Islands, as well as remodelling several others. The courses he designed included two at Richmond, Petworth, Raynes Park (sold for development in 1923), Sevenoaks, Tooting Bec, Walton-on-Thames, Wimbledon (extended), Woking and, of course, Surbiton, while Ganton (with Harry Vardon) and Lindrick, both in Yorkshire, rank among the top 30 golf courses in the British Isles according to some experts. Dunn himself thought that Broadstone and Meyrich Park, both in Dorset, were his greatest achievements.

There is no dispute that Tom Dunn designed Surbiton's original nine-hole course, and one can be almost certain that he was also responsible for the second nine holes when the course was extended two years later. We are fortunate that Lisner had the foresight to employ a designer of such eminence as Dunn, even though much of his original layout has had to be altered over the years as parts of the course were exchanged for other land for various reasons.

The Course of 1895–1897

Unfortunately, there does not appear to be any reliable and detailed record of how the original nine holes were laid out. However, from old maps and documents it is fairly clear that these nine holes covered very roughly much the same area of land, other than at the northern and eastern extremities, as where the present first eight holes of Surbiton are now located. The second nine holes, which were opened on 13th March, 1897, were created to the west of The Waffrons and to the south towards Claygate. The first account of the course I have been able to trace is dated May 1897; it is fragmentary to say the least and not explicit as is evident from the following:

The situation of the course is one of the most charming in Surrey, the highest points commanding magnificent views of the surrounding country. The formation of the ground is hilly, intersected here and there with ditches and hedges, which make good natural hazards, in conjunction with a plentiful stock of timber. The turf is excellent, and will improve with play; the putting greens are remarkably good, considering the short time they have been in use, while one does not encounter many bad lies throughout the course. Some of the new ground is a little rough, as might be expected, but plenty of tramping is all that is necessary to put that to rights. Several artificial sand bunkers have been made, but the number might with advantage be increased. The distances of the holes vary from 130 to 411 yards, the total length of the round being 4,541 yards. The 'Bogey' is 80.

A few words about bogey are appropriate at this point. This term was first used in 1891 by Hugh Rotherham as the 'ground score' of the Coventry course, and was subsequently adopted widely to mean the 'par' of a course; this meaning was formally recognised by the Royal and Ancient in 1910. Later, bogey fell into disuse in its original sense with the general adoption of the Standard Scratch Score (in 1925) and the assignment of 'par' to each hole. However, in the 1960s it came back into golfing parlance through its American use denoting one over par for any hole.

Tom Dunn, 1849–1902

Subsequent Developments

From the late 1890s through to circa 1924, the course underwent a number of changes. Unfortunately, it is not possible to pinpoint the sequence, dates and nature of these changes. However, with the invaluable help of Walter Bradley, and with the aid of some maps and leases of this period, it is possible to describe in approximate terms how the course had evolved by 1924 or thereabouts. Before doing so, it is necessary to mention what was probably the most significant event in the development of the game of golf which, inter alia, had consequential repercussions on the design and layout of courses throughout the world, including that at Surbiton.

Up until the middle of the last century the game was played with a 'feathery', a hand-stitched, leather ball stuffed with wet feathers which became very hard when the feathers dried out. These cost 3 to 4 shillings each, almost as much as the cost of a golf-club in those days.

The introduction in 1848 of the 'Gutta percha' ball, which was made by immersing rubber in hot water, rolling it by hand into a round ball and indenting the surface with a hammer, was a great improvement on the old feathery. The guttie was much cheaper, virtually indestructible, of consistent weight and size, with a more predictable behaviour. It is doubtful, however, if it flew any farther than the feathery. The longest recorded drive with a guttie, without assistance from the terrain or wind, was 235 yards. But it was the invention by an American, Coburn Haskell, in 1898 of a ball composed of elastic wound at tension round a rubber core which was to have the most far-reaching impact on the game. It was easier to hit and to control and, most important of all, travelled much longer distances than the feathery or the guttie. In 1902, Sandy Herd used it when winning The Open. Although at about 2s. 6d. it was more expensive than the guttie, it rapidly became the most used ball from the early 1900s, especially after Herd's success with it at The Open.

The main point of this very brief description of how the golf ball developed is that with its increasing acceptance and use in Britain, America and elsewhere, virtually every golf course in the world built before the arrival of the core-wound ball had to be redesigned and lengthened. Surbiton's 4,541 yard course was fine and challenging for the guttie, but was inadequate for the rubber-cored ball. When and how Tom Dunn's original course was lengthened, I do not know, but it is reasonable to assume that this was probably a little before or shortly after the Great War.

Many commentators consider that the development of the golf ball has been the single most important factor in the evolution of the game as we know it today, although some others would rank the introduction of steel-shafted clubs in the late 1890s as being almost as fundamental. Be that as it may, it is surprising how many amateur golfers equipped with a fine set of matched clubs are content to play several rounds with a ball which has seen better days, or to switch from one make or type of ball to another during a round without a moment's thought on the effect this may have on their performance!

Surbiton's Course from the mid-1920s

The significance of the above-mentioned reference to 1924 is that this was when certain land was exchanged in order that the Kingston By-Pass could be built; it was opened to the public in 1927. In a subsequent chapter extracts are quoted from Dai Rees's book which refer to the Kingston By-Pass being built in the mid 1930s. Rees must have been confused with some other major construction activities in the area, as certainly that section of the By-Pass which is to the north of the course in the general area of Hinchley Wood and the Dittons was opened in 1927.

Such evidence as exists suggests that the first four holes covered roughly the same area as they do today but not exactly so. For example, the first hole was not extended to its present length until 1957/58, while the fourth hole was much shorter at 147 yards until 1964 when it was extended to its current length of 188 yards. The fifth hole was a monster, and at over 600 yards, par-6, was, as mentioned earlier, reputed to be one of, if not the longest hole in England at that time. It stretched from the existing tee to the other side of the then non-existent Kingston By-Pass. Even after the By-Pass was built and the green perforce had to be moved to the south side of it, the fifth was still a daunting hole of 577 yards; it remained this length up until the early days of the last war.

Close to the original fifth green was the sixth tee. The sixth hole was about 250 to 260 yards in length with the green located just to the west of where the existing public footpath from the By-Pass to The Waffrons meets the course. In this corner, between the path and the houses of Claygate Lane, there is a flat area of fine grass with a few trees now growing on it – this is thought to be the site of the original sixth green. The seventh tee was in front of the present sixth tee, and its green was short of, and to the right of, the present sixth green. The sixth as we know it today was redesigned by the famous golfer, James Braid, after the last war and not without some problems during the construction of the green, problems which have tended to persist to this day due, one suspects, to the nature of the subsoil and the poor drainage conditions in this area.

The old eighth hole followed the line of the present seventh, but with the green sited short of the public footpath that now crosses the fairway. The ninth was a short hole, about 170 yards, with its tee close to the present sixth tee and with its green sited in the small paddock that is adjacent to the right-hand side of the present eighth tee. The old tenth hole was 372 yards, a little shorter but otherwise much the same as the existing eighth from the yellow tee. Was it such a demanding hole as it is today? – one can only speculate.

So to sum up this far, where we now have eight holes there used to be ten. All were somewhat shorter than the present holes, except the monster fifth.

The tee of the eleventh hole, which was 355 yards, was sited on the clubhouse side of the recently constructed ninth Medal tee. The fairway doglegged the grounds of The Waffrons to what is now the tenth green. Dai Rees, and a few of the tigers of his day, used to ignore this dogleg and drove straight over the trees and paddock at the green.

The twelfth hole, 450 yards, was also played as a dogleg from the front of the present twelfth tee, up to the left towards the existing ninth green, and then down to the right to the green. It was a different green from today in that it was only slightly higher than the adjoining seventeenth fairway where one's ball, helped by the slope, frequently came to rest. It was not until 1967 that the green was extended and raised at the back to its present height.

It would seem that the thirteenth hole has hardly changed since it was created, and while the fourteenth used to be shorter, it still hugged Old Claygate Lane on its western flank as it does today. Prior to 1937, the remaining holes were rather cramped and shorter, and in the case of the sixteenth and eighteenth, sited further to the west than is now the case. It was the exchange of land in July 1937, under an amendment to the Lease of 1932, that enabled the Club to redesign and create the more spacious layout that the Club's last five holes now enjoy. It was around this time that the fourteenth, fifteenth and sixteenth became known as the 'Claygate Loop'.

This description of what I have termed the old course, as distinct from the original course, is not precise nor necessarily entirely accurate in all respects, but I trust it will have given the reader a reasonable impression of the layout in the mid 1920s. Undoubtedly, many other changes of a less fundamental nature were made over the years, but details of these no longer exist.

Course Maintenance

For the first fifty years or so, Surbiton's greens and tees were cut by hand-propelled, lawn mowers and the sides of the tees trimmed with billhooks, as was the common practice in most golf clubs up until the last war or thereabouts, while the fairways and the semi-rough were cut by horse-drawn, gang mowers. In the case of Surbiton, its gang mower had to have the height of its cutters adjusted by hand every time it moved from fairway to rough. These and other course maintenance tasks were carried out by a ground staff of only four, if one excludes the help of sheep during the Club's initial years and during the war years as well.

After the last war, horse power, in the literal sense, was replaced by a small truck. But it was not until R. D. Ross's year of Captaincy, 1957/58, that Bill Adams, Ernest Newman and Walter Bradley, on behalf of the Club, purchased a modern (for its day) quintuple fairway gang mower from Swinley Forest G.C. This, together with the acquisition in the same year of a Ferguson tractor, a triple gang mower for the semi-rough and a Haytor rotary cutter for the rough, very quickly produced a considerable improvement to the course.

In subsequent years, further mechanical devices and equipment were introduced, a sprinkling system for greens and tees was installed in the Autumn of 1970, and these, together with modern fertilizers and dressings, have up-graded the course beyond all recognition. Add to that the tremendous advances in golf-clubs and balls and one begins to appreciate, even after allowing for the fact that the course was much shorter than it is today, how good a gross score in the 80s or early 90s really was for a Club member in earlier times. In this regard, the reader will ascertain from a later chapter than even the mighty golfer, J. H. Taylor, had to play his best using a guttie and wooden-shafted clubs to register a couple of rounds of 77 and 79 at Surbiton over a course which only measured some 4,500 yards in 1897.

The mention of Taylor brings to mind photographs of him and many other golfers of his day that I came across in various books and journals during my researches. With what is admittedly an unprofessional eye, it seemed to me that 70 years and more ago, the majority of golfers used the baseball grip before the Vardon grip became popular, and held the club in the palm of the hands and not in the fingers. Similarly, most golfers adopted a very wide, open stance when addressing the ball with the ball placed more towards the centre, or even a little to the right of one's stance, than is the usual practice today when using a wood off the tee. Both elbows bent, huge body turns, with the club head dropped well behind the back, were common features of the golf swing before the advent of the core-wound ball.

Putting was also rather different; again a wide, open stance was very common, with the ball more often than not struck opposite the right foot. Most golfers also bent very low, in fact some had their heads down almost to waist level.

All the men, virtually without exception, wore caps, jackets and collars and ties whatever the weather. But it is the ladies that catch one's eye, they too also wore hats, frequently straw boaters, while their dresses were invariably down to the ground, high to the neck, with long leg o'mutton sleeves. Showing an ankle during a swing was considered to be positively indecent. Yet they did, indeed in 1899 Molly Whigham recorded drives of 214 and 234 yards at Westward Ho! using a guttie, while Lady Margaret Scott, Ladies' Champion in 1893, 1894 and 1895, was a consistent long-hitter with a swing as full and as long as most men of her day. From time to time she showed a nifty right ankle, but as an aristocrat and a fine golfer she got away with it.

Some of these observations are culled from looking at many dozens of photographs; no doubt a more tutored eye would have detected other differences from the way we now address the ball and handle our clubs. These photographs, unfortunately I did not come across any of Surbiton of that era, also show how unkempt the rough was in those days, the broken and uneven nature of most fairways, while the putting greens at their best were more like a rather poorly prepared winter green. Given that many of these photographs were taken at the country's finest courses, one begins to wonder how a course like Surbiton would have looked say 80 years ago.

An Impartial Opinion of the Present Course

I thought I would conclude this particular chapter with some extracts from a much more recent description of the Club written for The Surrey County Magazine by John Andrisani in July 1982. If nothing else, it is a knowledgeable and impartial opinion, brief though it may be.

> *The course itself is different from so many of its Surrey neighbours which feature bumps, hollows, heather and fast rolling fairways. Surbiton is straightforward, with grass fairways and greens which are on a par with Home Park at nearby Hampton Court. Both boast what, I think, are some of the best greens in the County.*
>
> *You can score if you think strategically and don't try to bite off more than you can chew . . . I wasn't surprised to hear that James Braid, the long serving Walton Heath professional had designed the sixth hole, a 385 yard uphill design, featuring bunkers cunningly placed and a tricky green – both characteristics typical of the master's hand.*
>
> *My favourite hole on the front side is the 4th, a 188 yard, par-3, which though only a long iron from the tee, requires, to secure par, the negotiation of a severely sloping putting surface that can bring even the best of strokers to his knees. Augusta National has nothing on this one!*
>
> *I must agree with the Secretary that the 16th, an uphill 443 yards, par-4, featuring a narrow fairway with trees left and out of bounds right, and demanding the long approach to be carried all the way up the steep hill to the green, is the toughest hole on the course.*
>
> *How reassuring to have in our County a club of golfers who talk the game on and off the course, and review the score card at the 19th instead of the financial newspapers. What would be the point, I suppose, of the Surbiton members discussing business; they all know they have made a good investment.*

Interestingly, I played with a visiting Society in September 1986 and some of the members of this Society, who had never played at Surbiton before, said that the greens were among the best they had seen for many a day – a view shared by Andrisani it would seem, also by the unknown writer in his report of May 1897.

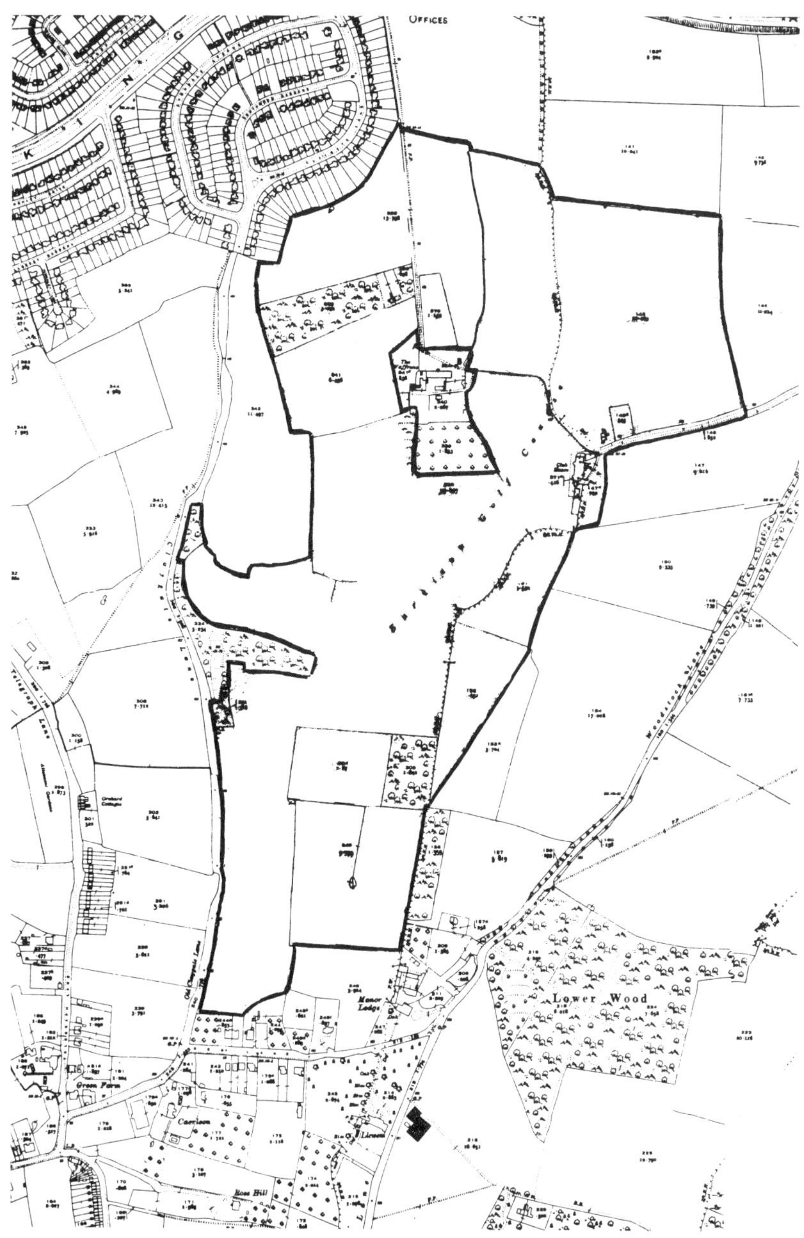

Surbiton Golf Club 1952

CHAPTER 6

NINETY YEARS ON: THE COURSE IN 1985/86

General Description

The course at Surbiton comprises 18 holes totalling 6,211 yards (5,676 metres) and as such just qualifies, by ten yards, for a Standard Scratch Score of 70. SSSs are decided basically on a course's overall length; for a 70 this is between 6,201 and 6,400 yards. Another definition is the score in which a scratch player is expected to go round the course, playing from the medal tees, in summer conditions.

Surbiton has twelve par-4 holes, four better than average par-3s, and two par-5s, with an outward half of 3,156 yards (2,884 metres), par 35, and an inward half of 3,055 yards (2,792 metres), par 35. Under the Rules of Golf, pars are set by a hole's yardage. Holes of up to 250 yards are invariably par threes, between 251 and 475 yards they are par fours, and holes of 476 yards or more are par fives. Par can also be defined as the score in which a first-class player should play a hole in summer conditions. The total of the par figures for each hole of a golf course does not necessarily have to coincide with the SSS, although it frequently does, and does so at Surbiton.

Starting is permitted from the ninth tee, in addition to the first, for some competitions and at stipulated times for general play. In front of the well-appointed clubhouse and the adjacent pro's shop, is an almost unique long and narrow practice putting green stretching the best part of 50 yards directly behind the first tee. And in front of the practice putting green is a huge double green, one of the few in England, that services both the 8th and 18th holes.

Unlike many Surrey courses with their humps, hollows, heather and fast-rolling fairways, Surbiton is a well-wooded, undulating course with grassy fairways. Its greens, with possibly one or two exceptions, compare favourably with many more renowned courses.

Surbiton, for a course located so close to the metropolis, is fortunate, as yet, in not being hemmed in by housing, industrial estates, or by busy, noisy roads. It enjoys a tranquil, relaxing atmosphere, undisturbed on most days by the noise of aircraft landing or taking off from Heathrow Airport which is but a few miles away. Once on the course, you are to all intents and purposes in the heart of the countryside, with no obvious distractions to ear or eye of a non-flora or fauna nature: it has many delightful vistas.

Probably its main drawback is the nature of the subsoil, solid clay, hence no heather and similar flora that can only really flourish on acid soils. Although for most of the year the course will generally be in very good playing condition, nevertheless during a long, dry spell, the fairways can become rather hard; while at the other extreme, after prolonged wet weather, the softness of the fairways means that 'preferred lies' are mandatory by Local Rule, which usually applies from late autumn through to April or even May. Some greens and tees can be somewhat slow to drain after heavy rainfall necessitating the provision of temporary greens and the employment of several alternative rubber-mat tees during winter months, a drawback which the Club is working hard to overcome. Slowly but surely these problems are being progressively eradicated, but it will take more time, money and hard work before they are entirely, if ever, conquered to everyone's satisfaction. But this having been said, it is very seldom that the course is closed for play, and even then rarely for more than a day or two after prolonged, adverse weather conditions.

In summary, Surbiton is a pleasant, undulating course of sufficient interest and challenge to test low handicap players and professionals, and yet not too difficult to dishearten those who are less proficient. So much for the generality of the course, its basic character and ambience.

It may seem precocious, to say the least, for a high handicap golfer to attempt to describe the course and its hazards in any detail, and more particularly to suggest how the course should be played. One can be almost certain that low handicap golfers and professionals will see it through rather different eyes. On the other hand, most golfing commentators are agreed that the majority of male golfers who play golf fairly regularly have handicaps of 18 or more – some suggest the percentage of such golfers is as high as 80. Certainly, Surbiton has its fair share of 18 plus members and visitors, so perhaps the following description may strike a sympathetic cord with many of my readers.

There are other difficulties. Although golf courses are created by man in the first instance, they are essentially living things. While Greens Committees decide where new trees and shrubs will be planted, and where the grass should be cut or not, it is Nature who always has the last word. She imposes her own challenges both in terms of how the flora matures, and as regards weather conditions which can change the character of a course in a matter of moments, sometimes several times during a round, while seasonal changes exert their more gradual influence as the year progresses.

With these rather obvious but necessary qualifications in mind, the following is the author's own impression of how he saw the course under what may be regarded as average conditions in the summer of 1985. Some months later the Handicap Committee reviewed the stroke index of the course because of the changes that have been made to it over the past years. This review resulted in a number of revisions which were introduced in May 1986. The indexes applicable from that date are given in parentheses for each hole.

A final point, while the holes of the course do not have any official names, several of them have been given names by some of the Club's older members for various reasons. These are noted against each hole, together with a brief explanation of their origin, while other holes which were not previously named have now been given names (with the agreement of the present and past Captains) for completeness sake. However, and to repeat, none of these names has official status.

The First - Ten Acre

Par 4, 400 yards (366 metres), stroke index 8 (8)

The first hole of most courses imposes its own special problems for many golfers. It is the player's first full strike at the ball, often in front of a watchful and critical audience, especially at Surbiton, where the first tee is very close to the clubhouse, the practice putting green, and the pathway to the alternative ninth tee. It is seldom that one stands on the first tee with only one's partner(s) for company.

The embarrassment of an indifferent tee shot is, of course, counter-balanced by the immense satisfaction of a well struck shot; all members have experienced both sensations from time to time. Otherwise the first hole is, or rather should be, relatively straightforward.

The fairway is quite broad and flat with no great problems, as yet, if one is a little wayward either to the left or right from the tee. However, a line of relatively young trees a few yards into the semi-rough on the right of the fairway will undoubtedly cause increasing difficulty as they mature in years to come. A really long drive, about 280 yards, may catch the 'L' shaped bunker to the right of the fairway, which also serves as a hazard for the third hole.

The approach to the largish circular green is guarded in the front by two small, shallow bunkers on the left and right-hand sides, and these in turn are flanked by several semi-mature conifers. These hazards only come into play if one's approach shot has to be taken at an angle to the green. The objective, therefore, is to strike a couple of longish and straightish shots, but with very little room behind the green before reaching out of bounds, there is a natural tendency to under-club and to be short of the green with one's second shot. Putting on this flat green should be fairly straightforward, although it does slope about one foot from front to rear which makes it difficult to stop second shots hit onto the green under fast, dry conditions.

From this description the first hole would seem to present no special problems, but for all that the author has personally scored fewer pars on this hole than on any other. First tee nerves, the inability to hit what is one's second shot of the round onto the green, or probably both?

The name 'Ten Acre' is derived from the ten acre field which, as mentioned in chapter 4, was acquired by the Club with the course in 1957.

The Second – The Gate

Par 4, 315 yards (288 metres), stroke index 15 (15)

After the traumas of the first hole, the second is less demanding. Any reasonable drive from the yellow or medal markers, which are on a common tee pointing to the right, should comfortably clear the long lateral grassy ridge that is about 125 yards from the tee, and which separates the rough from the start of the fairway.

The major hazards of this hole are the very narrow entrance to the green and the large, deep bunker that guards the front, left-hand side of the green. Not an easy bunker to splash out of if you happen to be on the forward slope. While a badly hooked drive or fairway shot can finish out of bounds along virtually the whole of the left-hand side of this hole, the right-hand side presents no such problem, although some scattered trees, and a small copse of silver birches about 75 yards from the green that separate this hole from the parallel third fairway, can often prevent a clear second shot to the green.

Probably the best drive for the less skilled player is to the right of centre of the fairway. This should give him a clear second shot to the green, avoiding the cavernous bunker on the left. The small grassy mounds on the front and to the right of the green can be a blessing or a curse, depending on whether they kick the ball to one's favour or not. And there is a little rough beyond the green to hold up the overhit shot to the green before it reaches more serious trouble.

The better and more confident player may, however, prefer the more direct route, pitching his ball over the bunker, rather than risk the unpredictable effect of the mounds to the right front of the green. Certainly there is sufficient landing area behind the bunker and before the green to make this a good alternative approach shot.

The appellation 'The Gate' relates to both the gate-like entrance to the green and the gate that leads to the lane behind the green.

The Third – Castle View

Par 4, 418 yards (382 metres), stroke index 4 (5)

This is a difficult hole to par, even for the low handicap player. It requires a good, longish, straight drive from the yellow or medal markers which share a common tee.

The first hazard is another lateral grassy ridge which is closer in than that on the second hole, but can nevertheless come into play as

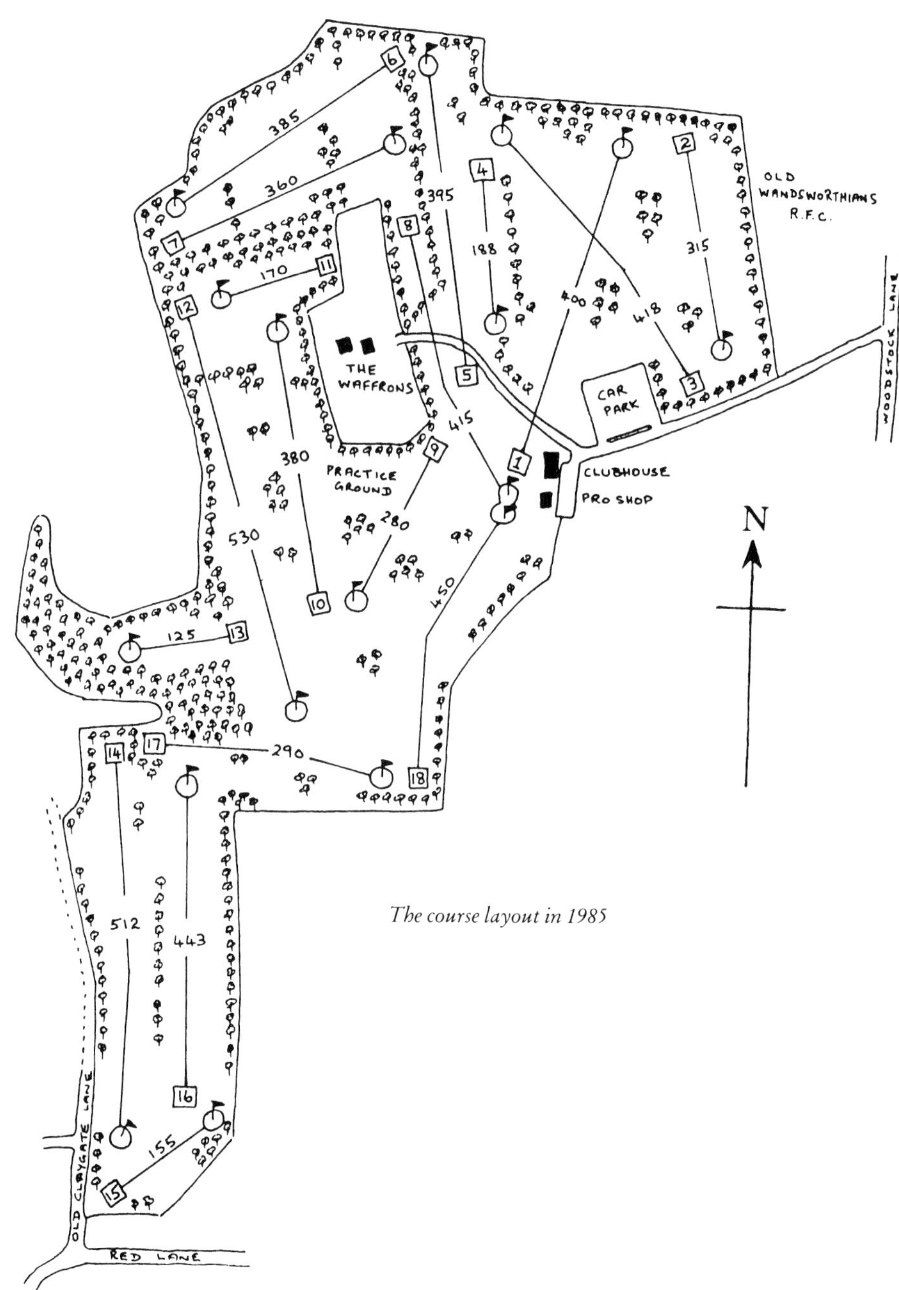

The course layout in 1985

the ground gradually rises to it from the tee. Between the tee and this ridge there is a small wood to the left, and a copse of silver birches to the right, but it requires a fairly severe hook or slice to catch these, and with luck one may still have a reasonable shot to play even in this copse.

The hazards for long drives are the two sand traps on the right of the fairway, one at about 200 yards, and the other at some 250 yards from the tee; there are also small woods opposite these bunkers on the left and right sides. Straight and long is the objective from this tee.

The green cannot be seen for one's second shot, even by the longest driver, as it lies in a hollow at the bottom of a downward slope beyond the first fairway over which this hole crosses. There is, of course, a white disc marker to aim at in the trees behind the green, but the precise position of the hole cannot necessarily be determined from this, and one must usually walk forward from the drive in order to see the flagstick.

The hazards for the second shot are the rough, including a grassy bunker, on the left, and for a really long shot, woods to the right which stretch around the right rear half of the green, and the big drop behind the green down to the fifth fairway. But many players will find themselves short rather than long on this particular hole, with the problem of judging how to pitch or chip from a downhill lie into the green. Equally, of course, this slope down to the green can sometimes give the player the satisfaction of finding that his ball has rolled down onto, or at least close to, the putting surface. The bowl-shaped nature of the green can also help to collect and roll a ball close to the stick.

As its stroke index implies (it was 4 and is now 5), it is not an easy hole, and one on which most players will be more than happy to record a par.

Players on the third hole take precedence over those playing the first where the two fairways cross.

On a clear day one can see Windsor Castle from this hole, hence 'Castle View'.

The Fourth – Willows

Par 3, 188 yards (172 metres), stroke index 11 (10)

The fourth is the longest par-3 of the course, and the most difficult. There is an intimidating line of mature trees and a ditch, a lateral water hazard, fairly tight in along virtually the whole of the left-hand side of this hole. The few small isolated trees scattered along the right side are not yet a major problem for the wayward tee shot, but will become more troublesome as they mature. More of a problem is the slope of the ground from left to right which, in spite of the lightish rough, can result under dry conditions in a misdirected tee shot slipping down on or close to the adjoining 5th fairway.

All this presupposes that one's tee shot has not made the green: never an easy shot, particularly against a strong head wind on this rather exposed hole which requires a good drive directed to the left-hand side of a sharply sloping green. Club selection is vital and can vary from a medium iron in still conditions to a wood against a stiff wind.

Three traps are positioned to catch tee shots which are a little short or long to the left of the green, while there are two deeper bunkers to pitch over if one's approach to the green is from the rough on the right.

Putting is very difficult from almost any part of this sloping green, with the easiest putt normally being played directly uphill from the right-hand side of the green.

'Willows' is a new name and reflects the fact that there are willow trees planted near this hole to assist drainage.

The Fifth - Waffrons

Par 4, 395 yards (361 metres), stroke index 13 (14)

A delightful hole with arguably the finest view, on a clear day, from any tee on the course. The long, narrow tee (both yellow and medal) gives one the impression of an aircraft carrier's launching deck. From the metalled track to The Waffrons, which crosses immediately in front of the tee, the ground falls away quite sharply to the fairway, which in its turn slopes from right to left for about two-thirds of its length. Some 200 yards from the tee is a prominent ridge running laterally across the fairway, but at a lower elevation than the tee.

While the tee is exposed, any wind is more often than not partly or wholly in the golfer's favour. A good drive, or a lesser struck blow with the help of a following wind, should catch the top, or better still the reverse side of the fairway ridge. Usually the ball will then continue to roll in a most satisfying manner towards the green, always provided it has landed on the right-hand side of the fairway. Drives to the centre, and more particularly to the left of the fairway, will frequently roll off into the rough making one's second shot to the green, which is guarded by a bunker on the left, a rather difficult shot to play as intended by the course designer. Even more to the left and you are in the trees, or worse still in a small stream (a water hazard) that runs through them.

So keep rightish most of the way. The green itself tends to slope from right to left to help entry from this side. It also slopes to a lesser extent from front to rear making it easy to run through the green under fast conditions. Perhaps the greatest hazard of this hole, with its prospect of a very long carry for a well hit, correctly directed drive, is the temptation for the less controlled golfer to swing really hard and give the ball everything he has got on the tee. And if he then tops, slices or hooks his drive, the green can seem a long, long, way off. But after a good drive one can be plucking out a shortish iron from the bag for the second shot to the green, and with luck a par or even better is a distinct prospect.

The name given to this hole is self-explanatory.

The Sixth – James Braid

Par 4, 385 yards (352 metres), stroke index 6 (3)

Assuming all went according to plan on the fifth, one will approach the sixth tee in good heart, but not without some trepidation. It was stroke index 6, but is now 3 which better reflects its difficulty in trying to score par. By any standards this is a tough hole which has become even more demanding with the recent construction of a two-tier green, and with the enlargement of a bunker to the right about 80 to 90 yards in front of the green.

Many golfers of medium to high handicap will, or perhaps should, play this hole as a par-5, and indeed they may not be too unhappy if they actually record a double-bogey. And because of the elevated green, the hole always plays a good bit longer than the fifth, even though it is in fact slightly shorter.

To the right of the fairway the rough is usually allowed to grow fairly long up to a ditch which is out of bounds. Just beyond the ditch are the gardens of some houses in Claygate Lane, Hinchley Wood. This is one of only two holes where housing backs on to the course, but not in an intrusive way as they are largely screened from sight by a line of mature trees just beyond the ditch. To the left of the fairway there is more rough and some scattered trees which separate the sixth fairway from the seventh. Down the middle from the tee is the target, and provided one's drive is fairly straight there is no problem on this quite wide and flat fairway.

The real difficulty lies with the second shot as towards the green the fairway narrows, with the added hazards of a bunker to the left about 110 yards from the green, another large bunker to the right about 20 yards or so nearer in, and a third positioned on the front left of the green. Assuming the first two bunkers are safely circumvented, there is still the challenge of getting up on to the upper tier, where the pin is usually placed, of this elevated green. Moreover, the upper tier is rather narrow from front to rear, with a bank and heavy rough behind it, and with out of bounds close in along the whole of the right-hand side, there is little margin for error.

With all these problems to tackle, many players will be content if their second shot lands up in the area between the two forward bunkers and the green, from where one can pitch up to either the first or second tier of the green as appropriate. Putting can be tricky, if one is on the wrong tier, but otherwise is reasonably straightforward.

The consensus of many members is that the sixth, with its recent bunker enlargement and the construction of a two-tier green, has become one of the four most difficult holes to par, an opinion that was obviously shared by the Handicap Committee when they made their revisions.

This hole is so named because it was redesigned by the famous golfer, James Braid.

From the fifth tee looking down to the green to the left, with the fourth green centre right, May 1986

The Seventh - The Slopes

Par 4, 360 yards (329 metres), stroke index 10 (11)

Close to the sixth green, but at a higher elevation, is the plateau tee of the seventh. The ground falls away sharply from the joint (yellow and medal) tee to the ladies' tee, and then on down to a lateral ditch, a water hazard, and some bushes before the start of the fairway.

Tight in along virtually the whole of the right-hand side of this hole is a dense wood, fronted by a ditch, both of which are out of bounds. To the left of the fairway, the rough contains a number of small trees and conifers which can prevent a clear second shot to the green. Nearer to the green on this side of the hole is a line of large trees at right angles to the fairway. These trees, bordered by a ditch, a water hazard, effectively guard the green if one's tee shot should happen to end up well into the rough, or farther over on the adjoining sixth fairway, a not infrequent occurrence if a golfer over-corrects for the intimidating out of bounds danger on the right.

As the fairway slopes from right to left for most of its length, the ideal tee shot should be aimed to the right half of the fairway so as to end up more or less on the centre of it. Direction rather than length is, therefore, of greater importance on this hole, with the result that some golfers will often opt for that wood or iron with which they feel most comfortable and confident, rather than risk their more wayward driver.

The sixth hole from about the middle of the fairway, May 1986

Assuming that these difficulties from the tee have been mastered, one's fairway shot, with the ball usually above one's feet, to the green has also to be accurate to avoid the two bunkers, one to the right a few yards in front of the green, and the other closer in on the left. The entrance to the green is fairly narrow, but the slightly bowl-shaped green should collect the lofted shot over the bunkers that lands on, or preferably a few yards in front of the green, if a straight chip and run shot is not feasible. The ground falls away both to the left and behind the green into heavy rough, often necessitating a carefully judged pitch back on to the green for the over-hit second shot.

Putting requires rather more skill and reading of the green than is apparent from a first, quick glance.

Straight hitters will enjoy and should gain considerable satisfaction in playing this not over-long par-4 hole, but habitual hookers or slicers may find it a somewhat greater challenge than the sixth on which to score a par.

A distinctive feature of this hole is the slope of the fairway, hence its name.

The Eighth - Bridle Path or Coleman's Watch

Par 4, 415 yards (378 metres), stroke index 2 (1)

The eighth is considered by many to be the most intimidating hole at Surbiton, if not the most difficult, a fact recognised by the Handicap Committee when they revised its index. All three tees are located in a long, narrow glade with a copse of mature trees close in to the left, and the out of bounds Waffrons's stables and paddock a few yards to the right. Forward from the tees is a high, thick hedge running obliquely right across the end of the glade. Whether from the men's or medal tees, the need to get the ball up and safely over this hedge to the fairway on the other side is much in the mind of the player as he shapes up on the tee. From the medal tee, which points to the right, the hedge seems higher and farther away than it really is - about 100 yards at its left extremity increasing to some 120 yards on the right. The tendency, consciously or unconsciously, is to try and hit the ball harder than usual, or than is in fact necessary, with the result that either the hedge, or the hazards to the left or right of the glade, claim quite a few tee shots every day.

If these problems are not enough, the fairway itself rises steeply from dead ground on the far side of the hedge to the metalled track to The Waffrons that crosses the fairway about 215 yards from the medal tee. As this slope usually kills the ball very quickly, it takes a really long drive to reach the more level part of the fairway beyond the track, which is at a higher elevation than any of the tees. Most golfers will be more than satisfied if their medal tee shot ends up somewhere on the fairway beyond the hedge and towards the track; and clearing the track to the fairway beyond from the forward ladies or men's tees is very satisfying, even for the accomplished golfer.

Assuming one is somewhere on the fairway below the track from the tee, this will almost always mean that one's second shot will be taken on a sloping lie with 200 yards plus remaining to the unsightable green - quite a challenge. The fairway beyond the track is broad and fairly flat, with a slight slope if anything from left to right, and with the green positioned towards the left-hand side of the fairway.

Entrance to the green is narrow, guarded on the left by the First Tee and a large bush, and on the right by two bunkers, one to the front, and the other close in to the right of the green. The green itself is huge, serving the 18th as well, undulating, and with a slope from left to right and from front to rear. So even if one is fortunate enough to reach the green in two, putting out is difficult from most positions.

The challenges of the eighth create two schools of thought, particularly for medal rounds. Should one start the round from the first, with its own inherent problems as previously discussed, and get the eighth out of the way during the outward half, or start from the ninth with the prospect perhaps of 'blowing' an otherwise good round on what is then the last hole? As a generalisation, higher handicap players probably tend to opt for the latter as being in their perception the lesser of two evils, while the more confident golfer is likely to prefer the former.

In summary, the eighth is one of those holes that not only tests the golfer's abilities to hit two good consecutive shots and to putt on an undulating green, but more particularly is a test of his golfing temperament and character – a test that many of us do not pass successfully very often!

The name 'Bridle Path' is self-evident. Its alternative, 'Coleman's Watch', comes from the many hours that Jim Coleman in his latter years as the Club's pro used to watch members playing up this hole to the clubhouse and his shop.

The Ninth - Crater

Par 4, 280 yards (256 metres), stroke index 16 (17)

Although the ninth is Surbiton's shortest par-4, it plays rather longer than its actual yardage. This is because the fairway slopes upwards over its total length from the tees to the green. Apart from the corner of one of the Waffrons's paddocks located to the right of the tees, it is impossible to get out of bounds on this hole. The main hazards for the wayward drive are a line of conifers leading to a small wood to the right of the fairway, and an old World War II wooded bomb crater to the left, both of these positioned at about the distance that a well-struck drive would travel on this rising terrain. Further over to the right is the Club's rather small practice ground, and to the left some rough and then the eighteenth fairway.

The crater is classified as a water hazard under Local Rules, although it is usually dry most times of the year. Hacking out of it is a very chancey business indeed, but the alternative of taking a penalty drop requires going back some distance if one is to attempt to clear the quite high trees surrounding the crater, assuming the intention is to go for the green.

From the original tees the green could be seen and was more or less directly in-line. This is no longer the case from the new, larger tee to the left of the old tees which was opened for play in 1986. Now the hole has become a slight dog-leg, with the crater coming much more into play than it did hitherto.

From virtually any point on the fairway it is difficult to judge one's second shot as there is no background to the green. The green itself is guarded by two bunkers. One on the left between the crater and the green, and the other closer in to the right. The green itself is effectively two-tier, although less pronounced in this respect than the sixth, with a steep forward slope. Judging length, up or downhill, is usually the main putting problem rather than direction.

Not a particularly difficult hole for the straight hitter, at least from the old tees, but a very pleasant one for all that which has become rather more testing from the new tee.

The name for this hole requires no further explanation.

The Tenth - Paddocks

Par 4, 380 yards (347 metres), stroke index 5 (6)

From the tees, which are to the right of the ninth green, and point to the right, the ground falls away gradually for about two-thirds of the length of this hole, and a little from left to right as well. To the left are two separate copses, one close to the joint yellow and medal tee, and the other about 150 yards from the medal tee on the edge of the fairway. To the right is the extremity of the practice ground, and behind it a paddock (out of bounds) fronted by a line of trees, which are quite reachable from the tee since the slope of the ground, and the cut surface of the practice ground, help to keep the ball running if you are unfortunate enough to slice it.

The tee shot should be to the left of centre of the fairway, as one too far to the right can end up in the rough and amongst the scattered trees on that side, with the paddock beyond.

One's second shot to the green, if it is from the centre of the fairway, should be directed at the flag, or perhaps a little to the left, depending on its position on this oval-shaped green. The green is guarded by a deepish, sharp-faced bunker to the right front, and by a shallower bunker on the left front. The green itself is pretty flat and long, with a small ridge circling the left and rear of it. Given a good, straightish drive, this hole can play rather easier than its stroke index would suggest.

Named from the paddocks of The Waffrons in which many a wayward drive from the tee has come to rest.

The Eleventh - Cottages

Par 3, 170 yards (155 metres), stroke index 12 (12)

It is uphill, semi-rough of course, all the way to the green from the tees, with trees for about one-third of the way on the left, and all the way on the right (out of bounds). The lateral bunker, some 50 yards in front of the green, has to be cleared from the medal tee, but it should not come into play from the separate and lower yellow tee which is to the right.

Either side of the sloping entrance to the green are large, high grassy mounds which taper down the sides to the rear of this oblong-shaped green. Tee shots which land on the inner slopes of these mounds will usually end up on the putting surface with a par or a birdie a real prospect. However, landing on the outer slopes of these humps, a matter of being but a degree or two off line from the tee, can spell trouble given the bunker on the left and the heavy rough on the right of these mounds.

For the correctly directed tee shot of the right length this is a straightforward hole, but easier said than done for many of us. On windy days, for example, with the wind usually coming from left to right, calculating the effect of wind on the flight of the ball through the air over the unprotected section of this hole is very difficult, especially as the tees are sheltered from any wind.

There used to be two cottages to the right of the tee until they were destroyed by bombs in the last war, hence the name given to this hole.

The Twelfth – Windy Ridge

Par 5, 530 yards (485 metres), stroke index 1 (9)

Surbiton's longest hole. The medal tee, which is located behind the eleventh green, is tucked into a corner with trees crowding in on it from the right. These trees, behind which is out of bounds, extend virtually along the whole of the right hand side of this hole, and can present a real hazard for the habitual slicer.

Some 70 yards or so in front of the medal tee is a head-high, lateral hedge. This marks the start of the broad fairway which rises progressively over about two-thirds of its length, before plateauing out and then dipping sharply to the large, oval-shaped, undulating green. Part-way up the fairway, about 210 yards from the back tee, are a couple of bunkers so placed as to catch any drives that are a little to the left or to the right of the central section of the fairway. 150 yards farther on is a bunker located in the centre of the fairway where it starts to plateau out. This trap, given the slope of the ground, can be a hazard even for the longish hitter if he doesn't get the ball up high enough. However, whether one is short of or over this bunker, club selection for one's third shot to the unseen green at the bottom of the reverse slope will be influenced by any wind and the ground conditions. Better to be short than long as there are only a few yards of roughish grass behind the green before the ground falls away abruptly to the seventeenth fairway.

All the foregoing presupposes three consecutive straightish hits, whereas there is, of course, rough and trees on either side of the fairway which, if found, can easily add a couple of strokes or more to anyone's score. Nor is putting a simple matter for those golfers whose ability to read a green is not their forte. Most golfers will be happy to record a par on this long hole. Higher handicap players will be content with a bogey, and perhaps not too displeased with a double bogey from the back tee.

There is another potential 'hazard' on this hole caused by those players who do not observe the Club's safety rules. Before going for the green, following matches must wait for the bell that those players in front of them must ring when they have cleared the green. The latter must then proceed to the thirteenth tee via a path through the wood. Unfortunately, all too often one or the other of these rules is ignored, not just by visitors, but by some Club members as well from time to time.

Prevailing winds, which tend to blow towards the tee, make this a rather exposed hole, particularly at its high point, a sort of Windy Ridge if you like.

The Thirteenth - The Glade

Par 3, 125 yards (114 metres), stroke index 18 (18)

This delightful hole, Surbiton's shortest, is almost completely encircled by trees. It is the hole usually selected for hole-in-one competitions by visiting societies and for Pro-Am meetings. As the stroke index implies, this is probably the easiest hole of the course, always provided one strikes a straight tee shot on to the green.

Club selection can vary from a wedge to a seven iron, depending partly on the position of the flag on this rather long, oblong-shaped green, and partly on whether there is any wind which can assist or hold up the flight of the ball as it rises above tree-top height.

In contradistinction, tee shots which fail to find the green are likely to encounter a variety of hazards. In front of the green there is a series of grassy humps which are designed to prevent the shortish shot rolling on to the green. Running down virtually the whole of the left-hand side of the green is a large bunker. And if one misses this bunker and goes farther to the left, the slope of the ground can result in real trouble, if one's ball doesn't hold up in the light rough and mole hills and rolls down into the trees and thick undergrowth beyond.

There is even less room for error to the right, but at least the small area of rough between the greenside bunker and bordering trees is flat which helps to hold the ball where it lands.

The green itself is not one of the best at Surbiton, and has tended to become water-logged rather easily and is slow to drain, but during the last year it has been much improved by drainage work. However, the main hazard of this hole is if one's slightly misdirected tee shot happens to land in either the left or the right bunker, both of which are quite sharply faced; it is all too simple to pitch out too strongly and to come out of one only to roll or pop straight into the other. I can recall one horrendous occasion of going from side to side, and in and out of each bunker, no less than three times to chalk up an inglorious nine for the hole.

All this having been said, more holes-in-one have been scored at the thirteenth than at any other hole at Surbiton.

This hole is located entirely with a glade, hence its name.

The Fourteenth - Claygate

Par 5, 512 yards (468 metres), stroke index 9 (4)

This hole is fairly straightforward, and provided you avoid going out of bounds anywhere along the right, neither the tee shot, nor one's second shot, should cause the average golfer any problems. If one tends to be wayward, then the answer is to try and keep left as there is the whole length of the parallel sixteenth fairway from which to recover. The two fairways are only separated by a narrow strip of lightish rough in which there are some scattered poplars and silver birches; better be on the sixteenth fairway perhaps than hacking around the roots of these trees.

The ground falls away from the recently extended tee to the fairway, which then rises gently until you reach the only bunker on this hole; this bunker is to the left, about 130 yards from the green. It is sited so as to catch the well-hit second shot of those players who keep to the left side of the fairway to avoid the risk of going out of bounds on the right.

Incidentally, behind the hedge which marks out of bounds, is the much over-grown Old Claygate Lane, now little more than a path which is just about passable in dry weather. It is difficult to visualise now that for very many years until the early part of the nineteenth century, this was part of the main, nay virtually the only thoroughfare between Claygate and Thames Ditton. It was along this lane that the products of Claygate's brickfields were carted to the 'port' of Thames Ditton, and along which the parishioners of Claygate trudged to worship at St. Nicholas, Thames Ditton, before Claygate built its own church, Holy Trinity, in 1840. Nowadays, the main users of this old lane are folk seeking lost balls - my dogs and I once found five in the space of half an hour; it is seldom the diligent searcher will go home empty-handed.

To return to the matter in hand, it needs two good hits to reach the above-mentioned bunker; most average length players will be a little short as a rule. Be that as it may, the green should be in range for one's third shot, the most difficult of the three to judge on this particular hole. This is because the fairway dips down to the green over the last 100 yards or so, and at the same time slopes from left to right. There are also a few silver birches to the right front of the green. The correct approach shot normally requires one to pitch the ball to the left front of the green, allowing the slope of the ground to carry the ball on to the putting surface. A low grassy ridge along the right and rear of this circular, bowl-shaped green should hold in the approach shot that is a little too strong, but in any case there is quite a lot of space to the left and rear of the green from which to recover.

It is perhaps the difficult - both as regards length and direction - third shot that has influenced the Handicap Committee to reduce its stroke index from 9 to 4. Opinions differ as to whether this revision was over generous as compared with, say, the twelfth.

This hole, running as it does towards Claygate and alongside Old Claygate Lane, is aptly named. It is also part of what is called the 'Claygate Loop', comprising the 14th, 15th and 16th.

The Fifteenth - Mount Ararat

Par 3, 155 yards (142 metres), stroke index 14 (13)

This is the only other hole which has a few houses (in Red Lane, Claygate) directly backing on to it, the tops of which can just be seen through the trees that border the right-hand side of this hole.

From the shared medal and yellow tee the ground rises quickly, after about 30 yards, and steeply, to the plateau green. Immediately in front of the forward sloping surface of the green, is a huge bunker with an almost vertical face. To avoid it from the tee is all-important as it requires confident sand play, or luck, or a mixture of both, to come out of it cleanly in one on to the putting surface. In fact if you end up close to or embedded in the face of this bunker, the only sensible shot may be to come out sideways and accept the loss of a stroke as being the lesser of two evils. Club selection on the tee is, therefore, critical; enough loft to clear the bunker, and yet enough length to reach the green, is the difficult decision to be made. This decision will be further complicated if there is a following or head wind. One never ceases to be surprised at the variety of clubs players select for this hole. They can vary from woods to a six or seven iron on the same day under similar conditions, and often they are utilised with equal success, or lack of success, as the case may be!

The green itself is flat, except for the front few yards which slope down towards the bunker. So even if you make the front of the green from the tee, there is the risk that when the putting surface is hard and dry, one's ball may still roll back tantalizingly into the bunker. The over-strong tee shot is perhaps the better bet of the two, as there is a five-foot high bank at the back of the green to help prevent the longer ball going out of bounds, a few yards beyond the green.

Tee shots to the right of the green are likely to end up either in a small wood of mature trees which, depending on the lie, may make a direct punched shot to the green very difficult, or if further right may finish out of bounds in the rear gardens of the Red Lane houses. Left of the green the ground falls away fairly steeply from right to left, so even if one's tee shot lands but a few yards off centre, it can roll away from the green ten, twenty or more yards.

The fifteenth is a super hole. It demands a straight tee shot of the right length and of sufficient loft at a small target area - do that, and the satisfaction is immense, with the anticipation of a birdie as one walks up the slope to the green eager to get a first glimpse of how close one is to the pin.

Hardly an extinct volcanic mountain or the resting place of Noah's Ark after the Flood, but somehow or the other the name, Mount Ararat, seems to suit this hole.

The Sixteenth - Telegraph View or Clover Leaf

Par 4, 443 yards (405 metres), stroke index 3 (2)

If the sixteenth has a fault, it is that the medal tee is rather close to the fifteenth green and well within range of a wayward tee shot to that green. As it is a Local Rule to give players on the fifteenth priority, waiting on the sixteenth tee for a following four-ball to tee off can be tedious at times. This does not apply on the separate yellow tee which is sited at a safe distance from the fifteenth. But the consolation for those waiting on the medal tee is the superb vista stretching out before them embracing virtually all of the fourteenth hole, Telegraph Hill, as well as the sixteenth itself and the woods beyond it.

From the tee, after a few yards of light rough, the broad, long fairway slopes down for about 200 yards, with a slight tilt most of the way from left to right, before it levels off briefly and rises thereafter to the green. Out of bounds, the ditch (and a small pond) fronting fields of Manor Farm, Claygate, extend the best part of 400 yards along the right-hand side of the hole from the tees; the yellow tee is normally sited close to this boundary.

The ideal shot from either tee is to the left of centre of the fairway so as to compensate for the fairway's crossways slope, and in order to keep clear of out of bounds on the right. Too far to the left will probably catch the line of trees that separate the fourteenth and sixteenth fairways, or if still more to the left, the fourteenth fairway itself; there is a small chance of hitting a tee shot long enough to reach out of bounds on the far side of the fourteenth. Some players appear to prefer playing this hole along the fourteenth fairway as a matter of routine, or so it would seem!

Some Club members regard the sixteenth as Surbiton's most challenging hole. To par it necessitates getting off the tee with a longish well-directed drive. Fortunately, the lie of the land helps, and in firm, good rolling conditions, this is one of the holes that even the average driver can reasonably expect to achieve close on a couple of hundred yards off the tee, more, probably, with a following wind.

Assuming this is achieved, it is the second shot which poses the real challenge even for the accomplished golfer.

In the middle of the fairway, about 100 yards from the green on rising ground, is a larger clover leaf-shaped bunker designed to trap fairway shots which are not sufficiently lofted. And with the ground continuing to rise beyond this bunker, some of the steam is inevitably taken out of a rolling ball even under quite firm conditions.

The right front of the green is guarded by a deep, sharp-faced bunker, sometimes forcing the less courageous golfer to aim for the left half of the green, rather than going directly for the pin if it is positioned on the right half of the green. While good golfers will aspire to reach the green in two, less proficient players will usually need to use their handicap allowance and take three, and be quite content if they are indeed on the green in three.

Some 10 to 15 yards behind the green is a wood, so the over-pitched shot to the green can well lead to trouble, but fortunately – in fact it is, of course, deliberately designed that way – the green is large enough to give one a fair degree of allowance in the length of one's shot before the wood comes into play. The slope of the green, from rear to front, also helps as no doubt the designer intended. Apart from this slope, and the lesser tilt from right to left, the putting surface is true and playable even under very wet conditions.

Anyone will be more than satisfied to leave the green with a four on his card, and very chuffed indeed with a birdie. A super hole, and in my humble opinion the pick of the course's par-4s, indeed perhaps the best hole of the course.

From the tee one has a good view of nearby Telegraph Hill, while the shape of the bunker in the centre of the fairway is very much like a Clover Leaf, hence its alternative names.

The Seventeenth – The Moat

Par 4, 290 yards (265 metres), stroke index 17 (16)

After the pressure of the sixteenth, this hole is a little more relaxing; Surbiton's second shortest par-4. Nevertheless, it still imposes its own difficulties. There is a wood tight along the left-hand side over the first 60 or 70 yards of its length from the joint medal and yellow tees, which may make some players aim more to the right than is necessary or desirable.

Some 60 yards from the tee a few trees jut out at right angles from the wood. Then there is a gap, a large solitary tree, followed by another larger gap which extends to a copse on the edge of the right-hand boundary. The ideal tee shot should go through this first gap, or over the tree, as the fairway beyond, although broad, tilts from left to right over the greater part of its length, before dipping down over the last 50 yards or so to the green. Too far to the right and one will certainly be in the rough, and quite possibly in or close to a small clump of trees and bushes a few yards off the fairway at about the distance a longish slice can travel. And for the long drive along the left-hand side of the fairway, there is a cunningly sited pot bunker that may thwart the big hitter. Just off the fairway on the opposite side to this pot bunker is a drainage ditch crossed by a footbridge. A ball lying in this ditch to the right of the bridge may be lifted and dropped without penalty.

Guarding the approach to the green from the right, is a sharp-faced, deep greenside bunker. While in front of the green, and running round the left-hand side to the rear of it, is a grassed-faced hollow – a moat if you like – with sloping sides. This hollow or moat serves two purposes; to help drain the green, and from the player's point of view, to try and prevent the chip and run second shot to the green, thus forcing the player to pitch directly on to the green. Ideally, therefore, the second shot should be pitched from the centre or left centre of the fairway at the flag with plenty of backspin so as to end up close to or in front of the pin. Better be before than behind the hole on this heavily contoured, two-tiered, sloping green, as putting uphill is usually easier to judge than a downhill putt for most golfers.

Since records were kept, at least five holes-in-one have been achieved on the seventeenth. These were by Messrs. Flew, Blanchard, Saunders, Pretsell and Windsor, but whether they were all struck from the medal tee is not clear. Digressing for a moment, the longest hole-in-one ever recorded was at the 480 yard, dog-leg fifth at Hope Country Club, Arkansas, by a Mr. L. Bruce in 1962, while another American, Norman Manley, holds the world's record number with 47 to date, including two in succession at par-4 holes in 1964 – it makes one think.

While no holes at Surbiton can be regarded as being 'easy' the seventeenth is one where the consistent player should expect to register a par under normal conditions. In poor weather it is not quite so straightforward as the green does not drain well, and putting is never simple on this contoured green at the best of times. In the autumn fallen leaves from nearby trees can be a real nuisance.

It is obvious from the above description why this hole is called The Moat.

The Eighteenth – Periscope or Duncan's Gap

Par 4, 450 yards (411 metres), stroke index 7 (7)

This is Surbiton's only real dog-leg. From the combined yellow and medal tees behind the seventeenth green, the ground rises to two grassy lateral ridges before the start of the fairway. A ditch, the first part of which has now been filled in, marks out of bounds along virtually the whole of the right-hand side of this hole. Beside the ditch is a line of mostly mature oak trees, with the fields of Manor Farm immediately behind. On occasion, these trees can be a blessing in disguise by deflecting balls back into play that would otherwise be out of bounds. Nevertheless, slicers beware, the snooker shot off a tree is not a skill that can be acquired – 3 off the tee is the usual outcome.

Going leftish from the tees presents no major hazard, although this will gradually become more difficult as the scattering of young trees to the left of the fairway mature. The real disadvantage of going left is the extra distance it adds to one's second shot, with the fairway dog-legging to the right after some 200 yards or so from the tees. Near the inside angle of the dog-leg is a bell to be rung after one's second shot to inform following matches that it is safe to tee off. From the bell the fairway slopes down all the way (about 220 yards) to the green in front of the clubhouse. This green is shared with the eighth, and has already been described.

So although this is Surbiton's longest par-4, if you have had a good tee shot and end up somewhere in the vicinity of the bell, a fairway wood down the centre should just about make it to the green with the help of the slope. As mentioned above, to the right is the out of bounds boundary ditch, and to the left front of the green there is a bunker to catch the misdirected second shot. There is also a shallow bunker between the eighteenth green and the practice putting green if you are over-long, with the out of bounds path surrounding the clubhouse behind that. For most golfers, the latter only become hazards if you need three shots to the green.

The eighteenth is a first-class, testing hole to finish a round, with a delightful view from the bell as one walks down the fairway to putt out, to be followed by a well-earned drink at the nineteenth.

The names for this hole require a little explanation. Periscope is what the older members used to call it from the periscope that stood next to the tee for many years up until the last war. The alternative is a post-war name after Duncan Smith who in his latter playing years found it difficult to make the fairway, unless he could run his drive through the gap between the two grassy ridges, which he did more often than not.

Some Concluding Thoughts

I have deliberately described the course in some detail, if only to record for posterity how it was laid out in the mid 1980s, and so that in years to come new members can look back and judge for themselves whether any changes that were subsequently introduced were for the better or worse. This is not to imply that major changes are currently being planned, but simply that the temptation for committees of most golf clubs to alter their courses from time to time is almost irresistible.

In the above description, it has been inferred that the relative difficulty of individual holes is reflected by its stroke index. This is not strictly true. By way of explanation, stroke index shows the holes at which strokes are given or received in match play, from one stroke upwards. Under the Rules of Golf, the sequence is decided by individual club committees with the object of apportioning the strokes as fairly as possible. Strokes are divided, as far as is possible, evenly between the two halves of nine holes. At Surbiton, for players starting at the ninth, the stroke indexes of the 18th and 8th are reversed.

At the beginning of this chapter it was made clear that how one might play the course was very much as seen through the eyes of an indifferent and erratic performer. This being so, I asked our professional, Paul Milton, to read through my draft and to correct any nonsenses; I am grateful for the various suggestions he made which I have endeavoured to incorporate to the best of my ability.

Finally, a word of apology to the ladies. Their view of the course will be somewhat different from the foregoing, especially as regards those holes where the ladies' tees are sited at a distance from the men's tees. For obvious reasons, the author cannot comment any further in this regard.

CHAPTER 7

THE CLUBHOUSE

The original clubhouse was a rather ugly affair comprising a single-storey wooden structure, fronted by a verandah, and roofed with corrugated metal sheets. It served the Club until 1912 when it was burnt to the ground.

The fire is reputed to have been caused deliberately by some women suffragettes. Why they set fire to it, if in fact they did, is not clear as membership of the Club was available to women from the day it was formed. However, membership rights for ladies in those days were very restricted and limited virtually to playing the course and the use of a small section of the clubhouse that was set aside for them - no mixed lounges in those days. Perhaps it was this lack of equal rights that stirred some ladies to take this extreme step, or maybe it was just part of their nationwide campaign to bring attention to their cause.

In this connection, it is worth recalling that the suffrage movement led by Mrs. Emmeline Pankhurst was very active around this time. It was not until 1918, after women have proved their worth in munition factories and other wartime activities, that some were granted the franchise; it was ten years later before women obtained equality with men as far as the right to vote is concerned. Rightly or wrongly, it was the suffragettes who shouldered the blame for the destruction of the Club's first clubhouse. Things have changed a lot since those days, but not without some struggles. Facilities for the Club's lady members have improved vastly over the years. Moreover, after some considerable debate in the 1950s, the ladies were initially permitted to use the main bar and lounge area in the evenings on certain days, and later this was followed by making this area available to them at all times on most days.

The replacement clubhouse was a more imposing and substantial building, although still largely built of wood on brick footings and with a brick-built chimney. Its principal architectural feature was an attractive white-painted verandah overlooking the first tee. Subsequently, a single-storey brick extension was built onto the northern end. This clubhouse was in its turn destroyed by fire in 1921. How this fire started is not recorded. All that survived was the brick-built chimney and the extension.

Every cloud has a silver lining and from the ashes rose a new clubhouse, an altogether vastly superior affair. It was built in brick, partly stucco rendered, with a thatched roof. It had a life of barely ten years before it too was largely destroyed by fire in 1931 when the roof was set alight by a spark from one of its three chimneys. Damage was very severe. All that remained after the fire was extinguished was its brick shell. The fire brigade did its best, but they were greatly hampered by an inadequate supply of water. Fortunately - if anything about a fire can be described as being fortunate - the fire occurred in daylight hours when there happened to be quite a lot of golfers, staff and caddies about. They were able to save much of the Club's furniture, effects and members' equipment before the fire really took hold.

The original clubhouse which was destroyed by fire in 1912

The new clubhouse, which is the one we have today, was very similar in its basic configuration to the old thatched roof clubhouse of the 1920s; the reconstruction took maximum advantage of the footings and standing walls that remained after the fire - a tiled roof was inevitable!

Incidentally, on each occasion the Club's insurers, Sun Insurance as they were then called, compensated the Club for the damage caused by these fires. As far as is known, there were no casualties.

Let us turn the clock back again for a moment. When the Club was formed, and for the next fifty years or so, membership was drawn principally from what might be termed the 'professional' class and included many Scotsmen. There may have been a few members who were tradesmen and manual workers, but such folk who were keen to play most probably joined clubs which, unlike Surbiton, ran a so-called artisan section.

The interior of the clubhouse reflected its membership. The walls of the lounge were festooned with stags' heads and other animals of the chase, stuffed fish and such objet d'art as the glass-cased, pendulum wall-clock presented to the Club by Col. Harrison-Hogge in 1915 which still ticks away in the dining area. Bill Farenden also remembers a fine ram's head over the mantelpiece which had its horns tipped with silver and had a silver snuff box mounted in its crown. Three stags' heads still hang in the lounge today, but mostly these relics from the past have gone, and the membership is now, of course, to all intents and purposes classless, in that what any member does for a living is his personal business and is relatively unimportant to the Club, and quite rightly so in this day and age.

The second clubhouse

Probably the biggest change made to the present clubhouse, ignoring the removal of many of the above-mentioned trappings and the various refurbishments that have been carried out over the years, was in the early 1980s. In 1979, the Captain, Ron Martin, and his Committee of the day, put it to the membership that some fundamental repairs and alterations had become virtually essential. Apart from renewing the electrical wiring, installing a better heating system and so on, the most important and costly of these proposals were the creation of a new and larger nineteenth hole bar, the building of an enlarged men's locker room, and the provision of new toilets and showers. Collectively, these improvements and alterations, including some not mentioned above, were estimated to cost about £74,000, part of which would be financed by a loan from the brewery. However, the greater part of the cost would have to be, and in fact was, financed by loans from the members themselves on the basis of a maximum loan from any member of £2,000, and with a minimum expected loan of £200. The scheme envisaged that members would have their subscriptions abated by £7 per annum for each £100 subscribed. Appropriate provisions were made for the repayment of members' loans under various conditions.

The second clubhouse after the fire of 1921

By end 1981/early 1982, these improvements to the clubhouse were completed and in service. The final cost, including some modifications to the original design, was nearly £89,000. Nobody who was a member before and after they were made can but agree that they have resulted in a tremendous improvement to the facilities and general ambience of the Club. Of no less importance has been the substantial fillip the new nineteenth hole bar has given to the Club's income. Increasingly in recent years, for convenience or whatever reason, members come up to the Club already dressed for play. The old pokey nineteenth hole was hardly an inducement to stay for a drink, and if the weather was not fine enough to sit outside, and if one didn't have the change of clothing necessary for the main lounge, folk tended to go home or to drink elsewhere. The Club must have forgone a lot of bar revenue in the 1970s before these improvements were made. To put it another way, gross bar profits in the two years after the new nineteenth hole was opened went up on average by some £6,000 per annum. More recently, in early 1987, the nineteenth hole bar was further improved by cladding the walls with attractive wood panels, installing a sound-absorbing ceiling, laying a new floor covering and by reupholstering the seats. This refurbishment has given the Club a nineteenth hole that is a pleasure to use and for which all concerned in its design and execution can be justly proud.

We live in an era of rapid change. Undoubtedly, there will be further modifications to the clubhouse and additions to its amenities in the coming years. Although change is inevitable, it is the hope of those presently responsible for Club affairs that sensible and civilised standards of dress and etiquette in and about the clubhouse will always be maintained.

The third clubhouse

The fire of 1931

After the 1931 fire

The present clubhouse: 1985

The men's bar in earlier times. Club members toasting Arthur Sturgeon after his hole in one at the fourth

The present mixed lounge bar which replaced the old men's bar

CHAPTER 8

CAPTAINS

The highest honour that any golf club can confer on one of its members is to elect him to the office of Captain. Strictly speaking, part of that statement is incorrect in that Captains of Surbiton, also Vice-Captains and Honorary Treasurers, are 'appointed' at Annual General Meetings; they are not elected in the accepted meaning of the word. Whereas all Committee Members have to be nominated and elected to the Committee by ballot vote of the members of the Club at an AGM, it is the Committee that 'recommends' to the AGM who should be appointed Captain. Thus the 'gift' of Captaincy lies essentially with the Committee, subject only to the endorsement of its recommendation by Club members. As a result, Captains of Surbiton are invariably appointed from the ranks of Committee Members. On balance, this is probably not a bad thing as if nothing else it helps to ensure that Captains before they are appointed have already had a pretty detailed and intimate exposure to the Club's affairs, and thus should be fully effective from the outset of their relatively short term in office.

If some members still feel that the procedure by which a Captain is appointed is not entirely democratic, they can take some comfort that the present system is a great improvement on the past, in particular before the office of Vice-Captain was created in 1962. To illustrate the point, Camm towards the end of his second term of office (1951) was asked by the Committee who he intended to propose as next year's Captain. He replied '*I've given it a lot of thought and have decided it would be better for the Club for me to carry on for another year*'. One suspects that some of Camm's predecessors may have behaved in a similar fashion.

But leaving aside these finer points of procedure, it is not just an honour to be made Captain, nor merely a recognition of past services rendered, nor of someone's playing ability; the post entails considerable responsibility, it can be immensely time-consuming, and, on occasion, somewhat of a drain on the incumbent's pocket. Above all else, it is the Captain who should, and almost invariably does, set the tone, general direction and conduct of a golf club during his term of office. This is not to belittle the time-consuming efforts of Committee Members, nor the vital and continuing roles that good Secretaries, Stewards, Greenkeepers and other staff play in ensuring that the administration of the club runs smoothly and efficiently and that the facilities and course are kept up to standard. Nevertheless, it is the

Captain who is the boss, the chairman if you like, of a 'company' which in the case of Surbiton G.C. currently comprises over 700 members with an annual gross income exceeding (in 1986) £200,000.

Before listing, for the sake of posterity, all past Captains of the Club, an attempt has been made to give a few cameo sketches of some of the Club's past Captains. These cameos, with the odd exception, are far from being comprehensive in their coverage, even for those Captains who held office in fairly recent years. However, this is not to imply in anyway whatsoever that those omitted contributed little, or left no impact during their term of office, but simply reflects the paucity of information available to the author, and no doubt the understandable reluctance of folk to talk about themselves and their friends and peers: my apologies for the inevitable incompleteness of what is recorded here, and also to those whose past achievements have of necessity gone unrecorded either below or elsewhere in this book. The following are not described in any particular order. Their terms of office are in fact from June of the year quoted to June of the following year.

Some Past Captains of Surbiton G.C.

B. Howell

Pride of place must surely be given to Bulmer Howell, not just because he was the Club's first Captain, but also because he held this office for four consecutive years (1895–1898 inclusive) – a record term which most probably will never be equalled.

It is reasonable to assume that Howell was a good friend of Lisner and that he 'managed' the golfing side of the Club in its initial years, while Lisner concerned himself more with administrative and financial matters. Although Howell does not feature very often in those few playing records of these early years that still exist, by all accounts he was a very fine golfer by any standard, playing to scratch at his peak. That is about the sum of my knowledge of Bulmer Howell, but these few facts speak for themselves.

Sir Alfred Mays-Smith

Mays-Smith, like Howell, was a founder member and had a great passion for motor cars and for the game of golf. He too was a great player who became sufficiently proficient at the game to play in The Amateur Championship on no less than four occasions; his performances in The Amateur are described in chapter 10.

Mays-Smith, or Sir Alfred as he subsequently became, was a Governor of the Polytechnic, the head of several important companies connected with the automobile industry, and was President of the Society of Motor Manufacturers and Traders from 1919 to 1921: a wealthy man who had residences at Oak Hill, Surbiton; at St. James's Street, S.W.1, and at Harley House, N.W.1. He was well-known in the golfing world of his day and was a member of Home Park G.C. as well as of Surbiton.

Mays-Smith was born in 1861 and died in 1931. He was Captain of Surbiton in 1900, 1909 and 1920.

Sir Sidney Camm, C.B.E.

Camm was arguably our most famous Captain (1948, 1951 and 1952), at least within living memory. He was, as many readers will recall, chief designer from 1925, and later, a director of Hawker Siddeley Group Limited. He will be remembered principally for designing the Hawker Hurricane fighter which served the country so well during the Battle of Britain, and later for designing the Hawker Hunter fighter. He was awarded the C.B.E. in 1941 and was knighted in 1953. He was a resident of Thames Ditton and died in 1966 at the age of 73.

At Surbiton, Sydney Camm (handicap 9/10) had the amiable habit of buying a new set of golf-clubs every month or so, or so it was said. Anyway he bought clubs very frequently, and many a member had the opportunity of buying an almost new set of clubs at bargain prices. Jim Coleman, always the business man, treated Camm's foible very seriously as indeed he might to his own advantage.

A partner recalls Camm spotting a young boy trying to fly an elastic-powered model plane near the sixth hole. Camm broke off the game and didn't rejoin his partner until he had showed the boy how to fly it, with a lesson in aerodynamics as well! Another remembers that Camm might leave the course part-way round and cycle home to his drawing board if some idea suddenly struck him. He was devoted to his wife, Hilda, but never played with her. On one Bank Holiday Monday he was drawn to play with his wife and created merry hell until someone kindly offered a swap to keep the peace! And in cycling up to the Club during the war years with Hilda, he always went a hundred yards or so in front of her all the way - devotion expresses itself in many ways!

By all accounts, Camm loved the Club and some say he did more for it than perhaps any other member. He was generous to an extreme, giving many wonderful prizes and gifts to those he thought deserved them. Although he was very temperamental and had a sharp tongue, he was at the same time shy and extremely courteous to the ladies.

G. Inglis

As Captain in 1939 and 1940, George Inglis is remembered with affection for his happy habit of dispensing free drinks, especially at Christmas time: a light-hearted titbit of a man who, more seriously, helped to keep the Club going through the war years. He was also largely responsible for the alterations made to the course in the late 1930s. His son, Ronnie, also a member of Surbiton, was a fine golfer being the Scottish Boys' Champion in 1937 and 1938.

N. Maclean

As Captain in 1941, Neil was another of the Club's wartime stalwarts remembered especially for the dances he organised during those difficult years – a man of great charm.

T. C. Price

Going further back in time, Tom Price was Captain in 1930. It would seem that he had his own special chair in the lounge bar – it is still there. Woe betide anyone sitting in Tom's chair when he arrived at the Club, as if caught, the penalty for the poor unfortunate soul was drinks all round.

W. H. White

Bill White, Captain in 1953, is remembered particularly for the effort he led in improving the standard of the course, which was in pretty poor shape by the early 1950s, with the rough as high as 'an elephant's eye', poor drainage and overgrown vegetation everywhere – a veritable muddy jungle in wet weather it would seem. He left Surbiton, along with several other eminent members, including Budge Gibson, Teddy French and Ron Layette, before the Club was purchased in 1957. These four all joined Tyrells Wood and all of them became Captains of that club in their time. However, Bill White's affections remained with Surbiton and when he died his ashes were scattered under the old beech tree that once stood alongside the eighteenth.

C. F. Hurlock

Charles Hurlock was, I am told, a big hitter of the ball. When he was Captain in 1954 he once drove his tee shot (off line) on the eighteenth into a pot bunker that used to be sited to the left of the fairway more or less opposite the bell. He was so enraged by this that he immediately exercised the full powers of his office and had this bunker filled in. Be that as it may, Charles Hurlock, like Bill White before him, was a very willing and hard worker who spent many hours organising and participating in gangs of members who carried out many maintenance tasks around the course.

The Hurlock family, including Charles, were better known as owners of the famous AC sports car works that used to be in Thames Ditton village. This firm, which was founded by John Weller in 1904, originally made three-wheeled, auto carriers – hence the name AC – which were bought by many London stores to carry their goods in. Subsequently, the firm was taken over by a Mr. S. F. Edge before it was acquired by the Hurlocks. Charles Hurlock died in 1969.

W. P. Beer

There are few members, if any, who have served the Club as well and as long as Percy Beer. Apart from one very short break, he gave his services unstintingly to the Club over a period of twenty-two years variously and severally as a Committee Member, a Trustee and a Director of Surbiton Golf Club Limited, until he retired from these positions in 1974. His year as Captain (1965) was notable for the considerable time and effort he devoted to his duties, and it was during his year of office that the present professional's shop and trolley shed were completed. In recognition of his past services, he now enjoys the privileges of being one of the Club's few Honorary Members, an honour richly deserved.

A. J. Sturgeon

Going back in time, Arthur Sturgeon, Captain in 1932 and 1933, was instrumental in establishing the competition that bears his name, which he won in 1935. It is said that he was one of the Club's outstanding Captains. On a lighter note, he is reputed to have kept for himself a bottle of cold tea under the bar counter from which he took his frequent nips of 'whiskey'.

J. M. Davie

John Davie, Captain in 1945, had the difficult job of starting to get the Club back on to a peacetime footing. A very good golfer who at various times won the Waffrons, Bradbury, Harrison-Hogge, Arthur Sturgeon and Victory Cups, the Captain's Prize, Gold Medal and Winter Foursomes – in fact his name appears on almost every honour board for those competitions that existed around the 1930s and 1940s. Davie was a stickler for observing the Rules of Golf and appeared to have had little time for Greens Committees. He is another of the Club's few Honorary Members.

L. S. Ellis and N. H. R. Adams

Although Leslie Ellis's predecessors and their Committees had put in a lot of effort in getting the course back into shape, there was still much to be done. In particular, worm casts were a major problem; the 5th fairway was particularly bad. Ellis (1959) led a drive of members to dig ditches for mole draining of the fairways and launched a 'Mud Fund' appeal which raised £336 for the purchase of over 4 tons of worm killer. This treatment was most successful and was carried on by Ellis's successor, Norman Adams (1960).

It was during Adams's Captaincy that the Club purchased the strip of woodland known as Smith's Hill between the 13th hole and the 14th and 17th tees for £300 at the suggestion of Sydney Camm and Alastair Craig, indeed they were prepared to buy it themselves for the Club if the Club hadn't.

A. Brinded

My reason for including Alex Brinded (1949) has little to do with golf. During the last war we happened to live in the same road, and I can recall as a young lad Alex and my father, who were both ARP Wardens, or was it the Home Guard, walking home together from the Stoneleigh Hotel during the height of an air raid with their tin hats protecting their precious bottles of beer rather than their heads. Men with the right priorities!

There are no records remaining of his Captaincy, but one can only imagine that all the immediate post-war Captains had a tough time in bringing the Club back up to scratch. Alex certainly had the greatest affection for the Club; he and Duncan Smith were co-founders of the Golden Balls Society. When Brinded died his ashes were scattered around the site of the old beech tree beside the 18th fairway, like Bill White, Duncan Smith and some others before him.

G. S. Mallinson and R. H. Avis

Gerald Mallinson, who joined the Club in 1955, became Captain in 1973. During his term of office he was instrumental in setting up an appeal fund which financed the planting of over 200 trees. In addition, the 5th tee was extended and a new 13th tee was built, while work was started on modernising the men's washing, shower and toilet facilities. These improvements, and more tree planting, were continued and completed under the guidance of his successor, Hugh Avis.

During these two years, there was the so-called oil crisis, and with inflation roaring ahead, there were huge increases in the cost of electricity, heating oil and rates. However, the careful stewardship of these two Captains, and their Committees, ensured that the Club's finances stayed in the black. In this connection, it is appropriate to mention that Gerald's son, Tony Mallinson, was the Honorary Treasurer during this difficult period.

W. R. Hall

Dick Hall, a charming and unassuming man, Captain in 1964, continues to be held in high regard by many members of his time. As Chairman of Surbiton Golf Club Limited from 1969 to 1974, and a Director for nine years, as well as serving as a Committee Member, Dick was an energetic worker for the Club during the greater part of the 1960s and 1970s. In all fairness, many other Captains and members have also filled these positions at various times with similar distinction, but to list them all would be a herculean task. Hopefully, these others will not take umbrage and will regard my selection of Dick Hall as one of several shining examples of the many good men who have served the Club unselfishly in this way.

During Dick's Captaincy, the 3rd green and 4th tee were extended and a new medal tee was built for the 12th, while considerable maintenance work and improvements to both the exterior and interior of the clubhouse were carried out.

R. W. Martin

Ron was one of the few members who became Captain more than once, his years being 1979 and 1981, after serving on various committees since 1965; he has been a Director of Surbiton Golf Club Limited since 1981. It was during his first term of office that plans were finally approved and work started on major alterations and extensions to the men's bar, locker room, kitchen, staff quarters and other amenities. This work was based on ideas generated and refined during the previous Captaincies of Peter Thurley (1977) and Jack Porter (1978).

Getting the members to approve the final designs and financing arrangements was not easy and required two Extraordinary General Meetings. It was during his second term that these extensions were completed and they quickly proved to be a great success with all members.

Ron Martin was instrumental, in 1963, in setting up the Epistles Golfing Society which has produced more than six Captains in its time. In 1964, as a contractor in his own right, Martin was involved, inter alia, in filling the large depression between the 3rd green and the 4th tee with 20,000 cubic yards of soil and rubble which enabled the 4th hole to be lengthened from 147 to 188 yards.

G. T. Fuge, O.B.E.

These thumbnail sketches of some of Surbiton's past Captains would be sadly lacking without a mention of Gilbert Fuge, Captain in 1985. It was he, during his term of office, that inspired the author to embark on this project. Gilbert, like some others past and present, has been, and continues to be, one of the pillars of strength on which the success and well-being of the Club depend. He has served the Club in several capacities over many years and is at present Chairman of Surbiton Golf Club Limited. During his Captaincy he was instrumental in introducing many improvements, and will be remembered especially for his genuine desire to meet, talk and socialise with as many members as possible. This is an important aspect of Club life and it is to be hoped that future Captains will follow Gilbert's example in cultivating a happy social atmosphere, in addition to their many other duties.

Some past Captains: Back Row, *Jack Porter (1969 & 1978), John Taylor (1983), Denis Squires (1980), Ron Martin (1979), Peter Thurley (1977), Percy Beer (1965), Bryan Lewis (1976), Freddie Pyrke (1955 & 1956):* Front Row, *John Davie (1945), Walter Randall (1975), Bob Wilson (1982), Hugh Avis (1974), Alastair Craig (1972)*

To repeat, the above are but a few comments on some of our past Captains. One among many omitted from the foregoing is Freddie Pyrke whose stirling efforts to save the Club in the late 1950s have been described elsewhere. Some others are similarly mentioned in chapters more appropriate to their personality or contribution.

Also omitted is any mention and recognition of those members who served as Directors, Trustees, Committee Members and Treasurers over the years, but for one reason or another never became Captain. In the final analysis, a Captain can only be as good as the support and

help he receives from these largely unsung stalwarts, but I am sure they will understand that space limitations preclude their mention by name or by deed.

CAPTAINS

1895	B. Howell
1896	B. Howell
1897	B. Howell
1898	B. Howell
1899	A. B. Tomkins
1900	Sir A. S. Mays-Smith
1901	C. H. Evans
1902	H. J. Stockton
1903	L. Reuss
1904	V. N. Douetil
1905	C. A. Hewitt
1906	R. Mould
1907	Col. J. Harrison-Hogge
1908	Col. J. Harrison-Hogge
1909	Sir A. S. Mays-Smith
1910	H. J. Hill
1911	W. Y. Johnstone
1912	R. Large
1913	J. A. E. Hickson
1914	F. J. Bell
1915	F. J. Bell
1916	S. J. Holford
1917	A. C. Barton
1918	J. Arnold Hill
1919	J. Arnold Hill
1920	Sir A.S. Mays-Smith
1921	H. Kidson
1922	R. H. Ferguson
1923	T. Stordy
1924	Dr. J. F. Weston
1925	E. Sherrard
1926	Capt. N. Y. Marriott
1927	H. B. Stroften
1928	C. H. Shuter
1929	Lt. Col. W. F. Ricardo, D.S.O.
1930	T. C. Price
1931	J. S. Dyson
1932	A. J. Sturgeon
1933	A. J. Sturgeon
1934	S. H. Titford
1935	G. T. Foxon, O.B.E.
1936	S. J. Holford
1937	S. L. Archbutt
1938	C. W. Daborn, O.B.E., M.C.
1939	G. Inglis
1940	G. Inglis
1941	N. Maclean
1942	L. Mason
1943	W. C. Hindson
1944	G. W. Shields
1945	J. M. Davie
1946	G. D. Rosser
1947	C. Cunningham
1948	S. Camm, C.B.E.
1949	A. Brinded
1950	H. A. Denney
1951	S. Camm, C.B.E.
1952	Sir Sydney Camm, C.B.E.
1953	W. H. White
1954	C. F. Hurlock
1955	F. E. Pyrke
1956	F. E. Pyrke
1957	R. D. Ross
1958	R. D. Ross
1959	L. S. Ellis
1960	N. H. R. Adams
1961	C. G. Williams
1962	C. G. Williams
1963	E. F. J. Baugh
1964	W. R. Hall
1965	W. P. Beer
1966	P. J. Gray
1967	S. H. Hewson
1968	Dr. J. W. T. Pretsell, M.C.
1969	W. J. Porter
1970	P. F. C. Weeks
1971	P. F. C. Weeks
1972	A. Craig
1973	G. S. Mallinson
1974	R. H. Avis
1975	W. A. Randall
1976	W. B. Lewis
1977	P. H. Thurley
1978	W. J. Porter
1979	R. W. Martin
1980	D. H. Squires
1981	R. W. Martin
1982	R. J. Wilson
1983	J. H. Taylor
1984	J. E. Harper
1985	G. T. Fuge, O.B.E.
1986	D. T. Blanchard

CHAPTER 9

COMPETITIONS, MATCHES AND SOCIETIES

In the final analysis, it is competitive golf which makes a golf club a 'club', and it is participating in competitions, irrespective of one's ability, that makes one a 'member' of such a club. Surbiton, like most other golf clubs, held Monthly (Silver) Medal competitions from the very beginning; it held its first Autumn Meeting in October 1895, and its first Spring Meeting in May 1896. These events have been held regularly ever since, except for a few enforced interruptions during the war years.

Surbiton's first no handicap limit cup competition, the forerunner it is thought of the handicap-limited Waffrons Cup, was held on Saturday, 4th July, 1896. Entrants competed for a 'Challenge Cup' presented by Percy Cavell of Langley Avenue, Surbiton. The competition was won by Dr. Norris with a score of 93–15 = 78. This cup was competed for for some years thereafter, but what was its final destiny, also that of any other cup competitions that may have existed prior to the creation of The Waffrons Cup in 1906, is not recorded.

What is known is that during the Club's initial years competitions comprised the aforesaid Silver Medals for ladies and gentlemen, which were played for on the first Saturday of each month, Gold Medals during the Spring and Autumn Meetings, and the above-mentioned Cavell or Challenge Cup which was competed for on the third Saturdays in January, April, July and October of each year. In addition, there was the Captain's Prize which comprised the best average of ten net scores during the season with no limit to the number of rounds that could be submitted for qualification.

In the September 1895 Silver Medal, W. Carr, a scratch player, had the distinction of setting the Club's first course record; this was a gross 38 over nine holes, a highly creditable performance by the standards and course conditions of the day.

Principal Trophies and Competitions

Subject to the foregoing qualifications, the Club's principal men's trophies and competitions, in order of their inception, but not necessarily of their perceived prestige, are:

— The Waffrons Challenge Cup: 1906
— Bradbury Challenge Cup: 1907

— The Harrison-Hogge Cup: 1908
— Captain's Prize: 1914
— Gold Medal (or Shearn Trophy): 1922
— Silver Medal: 1922
— Forden Challenge Cup: 1930
— Arthur Sturgeon Cup: 1934
— The Victory Cup: 1946
— Winter Foursomes (or the Coleman Cups): 1946
— Veterans' Cup: 1954
— Celebration Cups: 1958
— The Evans Trophy: 1962
— Robert Greenish Cup: 1962
— The Stewart Hewson Hole-in-One Trophy: 1971
— Summer Competition (or Summer Cup): 1979

All these cups and trophies are described a little later in this chapter, together with the names of those who presented them, the competitions concerned, and the names of all past winners.

In addition to the foregoing, there is a Bronze Medal for which the Monthly Medal winners of the Third Division (handicaps of 20 and above) over the previous 12 months are qualified to compete. There are also three important competitions for juvenile members – the Juvenile Trophy, also known as the Jack Porter Trophy, and the RAF Chessington Cup, both of which are 18 hole Stableford Singles, and the Norman Bell Trophy. The latter used to comprise the best 6 Medal cards out of 8 off the tees of the day during the summer holidays, but is now the best 3 out of 4 Medal cards. Ladies' trophies and competitions are described in chapter 14.

Medal Competitions

Important though the above competitions are to the Club and its members, it is the Monthly Medal which is the heart of competitive life in any golf club. While for many of us the chances of ever winning a major Club competition may be rather remote to say the least, most members stand a far better chance of putting together one really good round sometime during their playing career with the Club, and with a happy coincidence of skill and good fortune this may place him (or her) at the top of their handicap division. For many golfers the winning, if only once, of a Monthly Medal can be the highlight of their golfing life. It is the only competition which one can attempt a dozen times each year, or more if one includes the Monthly Mid-Week Medal. Sir Sydney Camm once said that he would rather have won a Monthly Medal at Surbiton than to have been awarded the prestigious Gold Medal of the Royal Aeronautical Society.

Medals also serve the vital function of establishing each player's handicap, and the base from which his or her handicap can be adjusted upwards or downwards as one's ability changes over time.

Surbiton's Medals have always been well supported – long may this continue.

The Club holds a Men's Medal on the first Saturday of each month, and a Mid-Week Medal which usually alternates monthly between Wednesdays and Thursdays. So far both these Medals have been almost invariably stroke play competitions with the former sub-divided, in more recent years, into three Divisions (scratch to 12, 13 to 19, and 20 plus): the ladies hold their Medals on the first Tuesday of each month.

Going back for a moment to earlier times, in particular to the years before the Great War, Monthly Medals were won frequently with net scores in the late 70s/early 80s, whereas today winning scores in the 60s tend to be the norm. For example, the Medal of June 1912 was won by E. H. Rusden with a score of 81–3 = 78. The next 13 places were all filled by single figure handicap players. Two of the tigers of those days, among others, were Mays-Smith (plus 1/2) and R. Large (plus 3); it would seem that the Club was not without its share of talented golfers in days gone by.

Other Competitions

During the year there are two Invitation Days, which are self-explanatory, also a variety of one-off special competitions, particularly on Bank Holiday Mondays, some of which may be dedicated to special causes or charities. The most important addition to these in recent years is the Charity Cup which is now competed for on a regular annual basis. This is a four-ball American Scramble competition over 18 holes for men's, ladies' or mixed teams. Its place in the Club's competition calendar has been recognised by the donation of four silver goblets for the winners which are dedicated to the memory of B. T. Wernham, a fine golfer who played to a one handicap at his peak. The proceeds from this competition, comprising entrance fees, a raffle and sponsorships by local firms, are donated to Cancer Research. Much of the credit for establishing this event must go to Freddie Burton: the 1986 Charity Cup day raised £2,100 for this worthy cause.

The Winter Foursomes deserves a special mention in that it too is rather different from the general run of Club competitions. It is unique in that at the annual Men's Dinner in October, when all the year's trophies are presented by the Captain of the day to the winners, an auction is held of each pair of entrants. It is the only official Club competition where members can recognise in a monetary sense their particular fancies. Ten per cent of the proceeds raised by this auction goes to the Club, while the remainder is divided on a percentage basis over the last eighteen, sometimes more, pairs that survive the earlier rounds of this knock-out competition. Pairs have the right to 'buy-in' for their own account one-half of that amount placed on them before the competition commences. In recent years these auctions have been conducted with admirable skill and good humour by Martin Nicholls, toastmaster extraordinary. Martin's consummate ability as a raconteur has been a feature of many of the Club's social events, while his son, also Martin (handicap 4), complements his father's talents on the course.

Matches

From its earliest days the Club has played matches against other golf clubs: of course the opponents have changed over the years as one would expect. The current fixture list includes matches against the Metropolitan Police, Banstead Downs, Wimbledon Park, Tyrrells Wood and Coombe Wood. However, the most prestigious match, without wishing to cause any offence to these and other worthy opponents, is that played annually against Malden Golf Club.

The Malden matches date back to 1937 when Surbiton G.C. took the place of Molesey Hurst G.C. after the latter had become defunct in 1936. The trophy played for, The Har-Myd Cup, and the winners of it, are detailed later in this chapter. Although Molesey Hurst G.C. was not founded until 1907, it is recorded that golf was played on Molesey Hurst – which was a fine stretch of meadow land alongside the Thames between East and West Molesey opposite Hampton village – at least as far back as 1758. In that year, the actor David Garrick invited Alexander Carlyle, Minister of Inveresk near Edinburgh, and some others, to dine with him at Hampton and to bring his golf clubs *'that we might play at that game on Molesey Hurst ... Immediately after we arrived we crossed (the river) to the golfing ground which was very good'.*

Like the men, the Ladies' Section has its own matches against such clubs as Wimbledon Park, Banstead, Kingswood, Malden, Leatherhead, Coombe Wood, Dorking, Sudbrook Park and Home Park. Even as far back as the years before the Great War, the ladies were doing battle with ladies from other clubs and competed regularly for the Miller Trophy against such clubs as Wimbledon Common, Raynes Park, until it was sold for development in 1923, and Leatherhead.

From time to time the Club has also arranged a number of individual exhibition matches with top professionals of the day. Most of these have gone unrecorded, but in chapter 11 an account is given of the first of such matches between J. H. Taylor and the Club's professional, G. Founds, in May 1897. Other famous professionals, including James Braid, Ted Ray and Arthur Havers, are known to have played against, or with, Jim Coleman at the Club during his time. The most recent match the Club hosted was on 21st May, 1986, between Ian Woosnam, fourth in the European 1986 Order of Merit with winnings of £111,798, and partnered by Peter Gill, against Paul Milton and Nigel Pimm of Surbiton. The result of this particular match was a one up victory for Woosnam (67) and Gill (73); their opponents' scores were Milton 72 and Pimm 70–2 = 68.

Ian Woosnam playing at Surbiton 21st May, 1986

Pro-Ams

Surbiton was perhaps a bit slow off the mark compared with some other clubs in introducing a Pro-Am Day, the first of which was held in 1979. However, since then they have grown from strength to strength and have become one of the highlights of the Club's competition calendar. As mentioned elsewhere, much of the credit for organising and introducing this event must go to the late Peter Webb.

Surbiton's Pro-Ams have attracted many high class professionals, some of whom were already or have since become household names like Ken Bousfield, Hugh Boyle, David Butler, Paul Way and Ken Norton – to name but a few, at random, from many. The event is part-sponsored by various local and national companies and organisations who offer a variety of monetary and other prizes. These, together with entry fees, can range from several hundred pounds for the top professional scores to cases of wine, whiskey and the like. There are also amateur prizes equivalent to various monetary amounts, and free holidays abroad and cars to be won if any competitor scores a hole in one at one of the par 3's. All in all it is usually an exciting day with perhaps forty or more professionals competing, each paired with an amateur guest of his choice, and matched by two amateurs from Surbiton G.C. The competition itself is an 18 hole, 4 ball, better ball Medal played on a handicap basis with the best two scores, professional or amateur, to count at each hole. Past winners have been:

Professional Winners

Year	Name	Club	Score
1979	C. Potts	Wentworth G.C.	69
1980	E. Stillwell	Croham Hurst G.C.	68
1981	P. Milton	Surbiton G.C.	67
1982	P. Milton	Surbiton G.C.	69
	G. Ritchie	Coombe Wood G.C.	69
1983	R. Whitehead	Moor Park G.C.	69
1984	P. Loxley	Effingham G.C.	70
	C. de Foy	Coombe Hill G.C.	70
	J. Garner	unattached	70
1985	L. Ross	Marlborough G.C.	68
	D. McLelland	Silvermere G.C.	68
1986	R. Whitehead	Moor Park G.C.	70

Nigel Pimm, May 1986

Pro-Am Team Amateur Winners

1979	J. Larcombe M. Hollands ?	1983	C. Nash L. Cook L. Greenhead
1980	P. Woodcock J. Gandar B. Lee	1984	R. Rice D. Way D. Lonie
1981	D. H. Squires R. W. Martin R. H. Avis	1985	R. Rice D. Way D. Lonie
1982	B. Marshall M. Nicholls D. Gillhespy	1986	M. Larner P. Sullivan C. Windsor

Professional Hole-in-One

1980	R. Richards	Leatherhead G.C.	£1,000
1981	A. King	Betchworth Park G.C.	£1,000
1983	T. Rattue	St. George's Hill G.C.	£5,000
1984	J. Luff	Surbiton G.C.	£6,250

It is pleasing to see that Surbiton's professionals have had several successes on their home ground, may they enjoy many more in the years to come.

Other Events and Societies

Other annual events include the England versus Scotland match which it is thought was started during the 1920s, and has been held every year since 1943, except for 1959. While it is no longer an official Club match, there exists a nice silver trophy called 'The Top Dog' which consists of a handsome Scottie dog mounted on a plinth on which most past winners are inscribed. According to the latter, England has won 25 times, Scotland 15 times and there have been 8 drawn matches, but the record is incomplete prior to 1934.

A more recent event is that between the Captain's team and the Vice-Captain's team which is a match held on Good Friday, and then there is the even more recent Four Nations Match which is a competition between teams representing England, Ireland, Wales and Scotland.

This is perhaps an appropriate place as any to mention a few other activities of Club members, which are not matches or events in the usual sense, but are or were groups of members who banded together in an informal way to compete with each other on a regular, friendly and informal basis. These include the so-called Golden Balls, the

Apostles and the Epistles Societies. Their main activity was to go away for two or three weekends a year to play on different courses around the country.

The Golden Balls Golf Society was formed in 1949 with a membership limited to twelve Club members. It was so named, I am told, after one of its founder members, the ubiquitous, one-time stockbroker, Duncan Smith, who gained a reputation for his skill and luck with the putter. The original members were Alex Brinded, a co-founder with Smith, Len Lofts, Jim Mitchell, Walter Rouse, Bill Farenden, Percy Beer, Athel Brewis, Eddy Church, Bernard Rowlands, Cyril Cunningham and Ted Middleton. After a good innings, the Golden Balls finally expired in the early 1970s. However, both the Apostles and the Epistles, which was started in 1963 by Ron Martin, are still going strong.

There have been, and still are, other less formal groupings of Club members who meet and play together regularly, but time and space limitations preclude further discussion of them on this occasion.

As previously mentioned, the rest of this chapter is devoted to listing the Club's principal competitions and the winners of them. From these the reader can ascertain for himself how certain members have tended to dominate some of these competitions for several years during their heydays. But before doing so, there is just one story among many that could be told that is worth recounting.

In the final of one of the Club's major competitions, probably the Bradbury Cup in 1936 or the Waffrons Cup in 1937, between Basil Kemsley (handicap 3/4) and Jack Physick (handicap 5/6), Jack had the honour at the thirteenth and holed out in one to the delight of the large gallery. After a while, Basil asked the gallery to be quiet so that he might take his shot. More noise and laughter followed as the crowd enjoyed the highly unlikely prospect of Basil halving the hole. But he shaped up, and to everyone's amazement he too holed out in one: incredibly the hole was indeed halved! Kemsley scored aces on at least three other occasions as have some other Club members such as Tony Stackwood and Jack Flew to name but two since records of this golfing feat were formally established with the creation of the Stewart Hewson Trophy.

THE WAFFRONS CHALLENGE CUP

Presented by: G. C. Sillar

Description: An attractive solid silver cup measuring about 10 inches in height and 8 inches in diameter with two handles mounted on its sides. The cup is engraved with the winners' names and the following inscription:

The Waffrons Challenge Cup
Presented by
G. C. Sillar

Competition: 18 hole, Match play, knock-out under handicap with a limit of 20 (before 1986 it was 18) and with a 36 hole final.

Winners

Year	Winner	Year	Winner
1906	C. A. Hewitt	1940	W. D. Farrington
1907	C. F. Nesham	1941	J. R. Jordan
1908	W. Y. Johnstone	1942	D. E. F. Alexander
1909	E. F. Wyer	1943	J. W. Young
1910	R. Large	1944	J. M. Davie
1911	J. Outhwaite	1945	H. A. Denny
1912	R. B. S. Banning	1946	H. A. Denny
1913	J. D. Drayson	1947	D. E. J. Smith
1914	H. G. Cockell	1948	S. H. Lewis
1915-18	Great War, no competitions	1949	I. C. Mitchell
1919	H. G. Cockell	1950	R. W. Greenish
1920	R. Large	1951	C. F. Hurlock
1921	F. R. Phipps	1952	C. Cunningham
1922	J. M. P. Furlonge	1953	A. G. Downes
1923	F. R. Phipps	1954	R. W. Greenish
1924	C. W. Measor	1955	C. F. Hurlock
1925	G. A. Reeve	1956	R. W. Greenish
1926	T. C. Price	1957	R. W. Greenish
1927	D. G. Fry	1958	C. G. Williams
1928	J. S. Dyson	1959	G. S. Mallinson
1929	D. G. Fry	1960	J. H. Spurr
1930	E. I. Scott	1961	C. H. Lees
1931	F. Ricardo	1962	G. S. Mallinson
1932	H. G. N. Cooper	1963	L. W. Welland
1933	C. S. Walker	1964	R. Harman
1934	W. Rose	1965	S. H. Hewson
1935	J. M. Davie	1966	J. K. Kane
1936	T. C. Price	1967	F. W. Girling
1937	J. S. Physick	1968	A. M. Stockton
1938	R. H. Allen	1969	F. Poynter
1939	L. Mason	1970	A. J. Cook

1971	F. C. Walker	1979	A. C. Bonfield
1972	A. G. Hutson	1980	M. C. Nicholls
1973	R. R. Langrish	1981	R. J. Hill
1974	D. L. Hyde	1982	A. C. Bonfield
1975	D. C. Davey	1983	J. L. Larcombe
1976	D. L. Hyde	1984	P. M. O'Connell
1977	M. L. Green	1985	J. Harvey
1978	J. P. Wight	1986	N. J. Pimm

The Men's trophies, 1986

BRADBURY CHALLENGE CUP

Presented by: The brothers and sisters of the late Walton Turner Bradbury who died on 17th September, 1906, as so inscribed on the back of the cup.

Description: A solid silver cup of traditional design measuring some 9 inches in height and 7½ inches in diameter, excluding its two handles. Winners' names are inscribed on a silver band around the cup's wooden plinth. The front of the cup is engraved with the words:

The Waffrons Golf Club
1907
Bradbury Challenge Cup

Competition: Singles Medal qualifying round of 18 holes off handicap. Best eight net scores qualify for match play. 36 hole final.

Winners

1907	W. R. Simpson
1908	A. D. Richardson
1909	W. B. Price
1910	R. Large
1911	R. Large
1912	H. J. Davenport
1913	C. Wreford-Browne
1914–18	Great War, no competitions
1919	Dr. J. F. Weston
1920	W. C. Tozer
1921	J. C. Durrant
1922	S. L. Archbutt
1923	B. R. Drover
1924	Sir A. Mays-Smith
1925	C. L. G. McKay-Forbes
1926	E. I. Scott
1927	C. G. Acheson-Gray
1928	T. C. Price
1929	A. J. Sturgeon
1930	F. Ricardo
1931	F. Ricardo
1932	F. Ricardo
1933	Dr. D. Macdonald
1934	C. S. Walker
1935	K. G. Haggis
1936	J. S. Physick
1937	H. W. Blackstone
1938	H. D. Allen
1939-44	No competitions
1945	J. M. Davie
1946	J. W. F. Humphrey
1947	F. E. Pyrke
1948	J. M. Davie
1949	G. K. W. Stead
1950	J. W. F. Humphrey
1951	E. J. McLeod
1952	Dr. J. W. T. Pretsell, M.C.
1953	Dr. D. Macdonald
1954	J. M. Davie
1955	P. J. Gray
1956	C. G. Williams
1957	B. Wernham
1958	B. Wernham
1959	E. J. Jones
1960	B. DeVetta
1961	D. T. Blanchard
1962	F. Long
1963	D. H. Squires
1964	A. Tarring
1965	D. T. Wernham
1966	F. Long
1967	A. J. Cook
1968	D. H. Squires
1969	F. Poynter
1970	D. G. Kirk
1971	Dr. J. W. T. Pretsell, M.C.

1972	D. E. Gillhespy	1980	I. J. S. Mather
1973	C. Gledhill	1981	R. J. Hill
1974	D. L. Hyde	1982	M. J. Froud
1975	D. T. Blanchard	1983	M. C. Nicholls
1976	J. Hill	1984	G. S. Mallinson
1977	A G. Hutson	1985	J. Flew
1978	A. P. Witt	1986	M. E. Pearce
1979	J. N. Tyrrell		

THE HARRISON-HOGGE CUP

Presented by: Col. J. H. Harrison-Hogge

Description: A solid silver bowl of about 8½ inches in height and 10 inches in diameter. It is engraved with the winners' names and the following inscription:

Surbiton Golf Club
Captain's Prize
26th September 1908
Presented by
Col. J. H. Harrison-Hogge

Competition: 36 hole Medal play, handicap limit 20.

Winners

1908	C. H. Evans	1934	B. F. Withey
1909	B. A. Beer	1935	J. R. Jordon
1910	R. Large	1936	R. G. Inglis
1911	F. Suttaford	1937	G. D. Rosser
1912	E. C. Peglar	1938	M. R. Moritz
1913	W. Upward	1939	J. M. Davie
1914	J. C. Cox	1940-44	No competitions
1915-18	Great War, no competitions	1945	B. A Kemsley
1919	K. H. S. Clarke	1946	A. J. Bott
1920	R. W. Stevenson	1947	W. P. Beer
1921	F. H. Ritchie	1948	H. A. Denney
1922	Dr. A. J. Foote	1949	F. J. Tovey
1923	Capt. C. G. Mitchell	1950	W. P. Beer
1924	Dr. A. V. Moberly	1951	P. F. C. Weeks
1925	F. A. Hickson	1952	R. J. W. Grieve
1926	J. W. Beare	1953	T. A. W. Rouse
1927	B. R. Drover	1954	W. H. Lewis
1928	H. Kidson	1955	W. R. Hall
1929	J. W. Young	1956	E. S. Lovegrove
1930	S. L. Archbutt	1957	J. C. Pether
1931	A. D. S. Gordon	1958	J. H. Spurr
1932	H. A. Butterfield	1959	P. J. Shepherd
1933	K. G. Haggis	1960	P. J. Gray

1961	P. H. Hawker	1974	A. Heather
1962	P. H. Hawker	1975	A. G. Hutson
1963	D. H. Squires	1976	R. M. Sandford
1964	W. F. Holmes	1977	J. P. Latham
1965	D. T. Blanchard	1978	D. T. Blanchard
1966	P. G. East	1979	J. K. Maddin
1967	A. J. Cook	1980	R. Rice
1968	C. H. Hustwick	1981	R. C. Anderson
1969	C. H. Hustwick	1982	R. G. Fletcher
1970	D. W. White	1983	P. M. O'Connell
1971	A. J. Cook	1984	A. H. Cree
1972	A. Heather	1985	P. Bloxham
1973	D. T. Blanchard	1986	S. M. Freeman

CAPTAIN'S PRIZE

Presented by: The Captain of the day.

Description: The actual prize is that selected by the Captain of the day.

Competition: At the discretion of the Captain of the day but usually 18 hole Medal play.

Winners

1914	J. M. P. Furlonge	1941	L. Mason
1915-18	Great War, no competitions	1942	J. M. Davie
1919	H. G. Cockell	1943	C. S. Walker
1920	R. H. Ferguson	1944	J. S. Perry
1921	J. M. P. Furlonge	1945	W. J. Kitto
1922	J. W. Brigden	1946	S. H. Lewis
1923	A. S. Mays-Smith	1947	P. N. Kitching
1924	S. L. Archbutt	1948	J. M. Davie
1925	A. D. S. Gordon	1949	W. P. Beer
1926	Dr. A. J. Foote	1950	R. W. Greenish
1927	F. D. Rae	1951	C. Cunningham
1928	S. L. Archbutt	1952	Dr. J. W. T. Pretsell, M.C.
1929	S. H. Titford	1953	L. J. Menzies
1930	A. D. S. Gordon	1954	G. S. Mallinson
1931	Dr. F. Carson	1955	R. W. Greenish
1932	Dr. F. Carson	1956	D. W. Browse
1933	Dr. D. Macdonald	1957	L. S. Ellis
1934	W. H. Page	1958	L. W. Welland
1935	R. O. Sherrard	1959	D. K. Beale
1936	S. H. Laker	1960	J. Hutchinson
1937	S. H. Lewis	1961	S. H. Hewson
1938	A. Dilnot	1962	S. R. Wood
1939	S. H. Lewis	1963	P. G. East
1940	S. Camm	1964	W. P. Beer

1965	L. W. Welland	1976	G. Bussicott
1966	B. T. Wernham	1977	J. A. Kemp
1967	M. L. Green	1978	J. K. Saunders
1968	F. Clements	1979	T. E. Fry
1969	R. R. Langrish	1980	J. M. Rae
1970	S. H. Brain	1981	B. C. Munro
1971	D. L. Hyde	1982	R. W. Smith
1972	A. D. Lacey	1983	R. G. Fletcher
1973	N. H. Green	1984	J. T. Humphries
1974	C. A. Pink	1985	S. R. Smith
1975	D. C. Davey	1986	K. L. Larcombe

GOLD MEDAL
(also known as the Shearn Trophy)

Presented by: Norman Shearn when he left the Club to live in New Zealand.

Description: This is a traditional name for this particular type of competition, although the trophy in this instance is a 10 inch diameter silver salver and not a gold medal. The salver is inscribed:

The Surbiton Golf Club
Presented by
Mr. N. W. Shearn

Competition: A play off between the monthly Medal winners over the previous twelve months in the first division (i.e. handicaps of 12 and less).

Winners

1922	Dr. J. F. Weston	1939	A. W. Page
1923	H. Kidson	1940-46	No competitions
1924	A. D. S. Gordon	1947	C. S. Walker
1925	G. E. Coppard	1948	W. H. Kitching
1926	B. R. Drover	1949	C. F. Hurlock
1927	C. L. G. McKay-Forbes	1950	R. W. Greenish
1928	G. A. Reeve	1951	W. H. White
1929	F. D. Rae	1952	W. R. Robertson
1930	Dr. F. Carson	1953	R. W. Greenish
1931	J. D. Hossack	1954	R. Bryant
1932	No competition	1955	R. Bryant
1933	K. M. Wood	1956	Dr. D. J. Cussen
1934	A. D. S. Gordon	1957	Dr. J. W. T. Pretsell, M.C.
1935	A. T. Redgwell	1958	W. P. Beer
1936	T. C. Price	1959	E. J. Jones
1937	H. D. Allen	1960	S. R. Wood
1938	J. M. Davie	1961	S. R. Wood

1962	D. G. Moore
1963	P. H. Hawker
1964	J. M. Rae
1965	A. R. P. Briant
1966	F. Clements
1967	M. L. Green
1968	B. T. Wernham
1969	B. T. Wernham
1970	D. G. Moore
1971	R. Wood
1972	M. L. Green
1973	W. J. S. Lovett
1974	P. J. Bromhead
1975	A. G. Hutson
1976	R. A. Schooley
1977	S. G. Fry
1978	G. P. White
1979	A. P. Witt
1980	I. J. S. Mather
1981	G. W. Hoskin
1982	P. O'Connell
1983	W. J. Da Costa
1984	J. A. H. Ayris
1985	J. P. Moss
1986	R. M. Sandford

SILVER MEDAL

Competition: Monthly Medal winners of the Second Division (handicaps from 13 to 19) over the previous 12 months are qualified to compete.

Winners

1922	G. E. Hickman
1923	R. Ridding
1924	C. L. G. McKay-Forbes
1925	H. F. Buckingham
1926	E. M. Taylor
1927	H. B. Strofton
1928	J. Hill
1929	R. O. Sherrard
1930	R. O. Sherrard
1931	A. J. Stevenson
1932	—
1933	J. R. Jordan
1934	E. E. King
1935	G. Inglis
1936	H. D. Allen
1937	N. Maclean
1938	H. W. Blackstone
1939	A. W. Newton
1940-46	No competitions
1947	W. P. Beer
1948	S. C. Mylam
1949	A. J. Mackenzie
1950	H. W. Roundtree
1951	J. V. Church
1952	A. W. J. Coxon
1953	R. G. Evans
1954	A. Rhiando
1955	W. H. Lewis
1956	W. H. Lewis
1957	E. B. Gillhespy
1958	J. Gowers
1959	C. E. Payne
1960	G. Milne
1961	A. R. P. Briant
1962	G. Milne
1963	W. A. J. Robbins
1964	J. H. M. Flew
1965	H. L. Moore
1966	J. T. Cook
1967	Dr. D. MacDonald
1968	I. P. Rose
1969	D. W. White
1970	G. E. Lewis
1971	M. P. Parkes
1972	E. Gillhespy
1973	P. J. Bromhead
1974	P. J. Bromhead
1975	R. A. Schooley
1976	A. E. K. Webber
1977	W. J. Kinstrie
1978	D. Fenwick
1979	G. H. Pegler
1980	J. H. Blackmore
1981	P. M. O'Connell
1982	R. W. Smith
1983	A. Hammond
1984	J. A. Kemp
1985	S. R. Smith
1986	L. C. Linscott

THE 'HAR-MYD' CUP

Presented by: A. N. Harper and C. W. Myddleton of Malden Golf Club in 1926.

Description: This solid silver cup of traditional shape and design is $9\frac{1}{2}$ inches high, with a diameter, excluding the two handles mounted on either side, of about 6 inches.

Competition: Between 1926 and 1935 this cup was competed for annually by Malden Golf Club and Molesey Hurst Golf Club. With the demise of the latter Club in 1936, Surbiton took the place of Molesey Hurst in 1937. The venue of this all-day match alternates between the two Clubs with the home team matching the unlimited entries of the visiting Club.

Winners

1926	Molesey Hurst G.C.	1933	Malden
1927	Malden G.C.	1934	Molesey Hurst
1928	Molesey Hurst	1935	Malden
1929	Malden	1936	Not held
1930	Molesey Hurst	1937	Surbiton G. C.
1931	Malden	1938	Surbiton
1932	Malden	1939	Malden

Dick Hall, Captain of Surbiton, retaining the 'Har-Myd' Cup in 1964 – the Captain of Malden is on the right

1940-51	No contests	1969	Malden
1952	Surbiton	1970	Surbiton
1953	Malden	1971	Malden
1954	Surbiton	1972	Surbiton
1955	Malden	1973	Malden
1956	Malden	1974	Surbiton
1957	Surbiton	1975	Malden
1958	Malden	1976	Malden
1959	Surbiton	1977	Malden
1960	Surbiton	1978	Surbiton
1961	Malden	1979	Malden
1962	Malden	1980	Malden
1963	Surbiton	1981	Malden
1964	Surbiton	1982	Surbiton
1965	Malden	1983	Surbiton
1966	Surbiton	1984	Surbiton
1967	Malden	1985	Surbiton
1968	Surbiton	1986	Surbiton

FORDEN CHALLENGE CUP

Presented by: James Ford and Frank B. Dehn

Description: A shallow, bowl-shaped, solid silver cup of 6½ inches diameter, mounted on a slender column with a 4 inch circular base. There are two curved handles attached to the lip of the bowl and to the sides of the column. The overall height of this trophy, excluding its plinth, is 8½ inches.

Competition: A singles Match play competition over 18 holes. Originally for members with handicaps of 18 and over, but in 1986 the limit was raised to 20. Full difference of handicap is allowed; previous winners are not eligible.

Winners

1930	C. Birch	1943	H. Owen
1931	Dr. D. Macdonald	1944	W. A. Roffey
1932	C. H. Jupp	1945	C. F. Scott
1933	J. A. Goddard	1946	T. E. Newman
1934	M. R. Moritz	1947	F. E. Pyrke
1935	C. W. Ruttledge	1948	S. D. Heal
1936	R. J. Pritchard	1949	A. Hughes
1937	B. Burd	1950	A. C. Richards
1938	S. Zan-Giacomi	1951	R. Bryant
1939	R. A. Moore	1952	D. E. J. Smith
1940	W. H. Scamell	1953	J. H. Biddle
1941	F. L. Summerhayes	1954	W. D. Munrow
1942	P. H. McCann	1955	E. J. Jones

1956	J. H. Spurr
1957	M. J. Hynes
1958	C. E. Payne
1959	S. H. Brain
1960	R. H. Avis
1961	F. De Vetta
1962	M. J. Prince
1963	R. W. Martin
1964	J. E. Harper
1965	F. Clements
1966	D. D. Brant
1967	E. D. Peacock
1968	G. H. Pegler
1969	K. J. Winton
1970	C. A. F. Jones
1971	W. J. Mitchell
1972	I. R. Gillhespy
1973	R. E. Baker
1974	P. J. T. Webb
1975	K. B. G. Hibbs
1976	L. Perry
1977	J. T. Ramage
1978	W. E. Brough
1979	J. M. Clews
1980	A. H. Mallinson
1981	J. Elliott
1982	E. Trevithick
1983	N. Spearing
1984	P. I. Griffiths
1985	C. E. J. Capp
1986	M. E. Pearce

Arthur Sturgeon Cup Meeting 1954
L-R *Tom Price*, John Davie*, Glyn Rosser*, Charles Hurlock, Sydney Archbutt*, Harry Denny*, George Inglis, Neil McLean*, Garnet Shields, Sydney Camm*, Willy Hindson*, Bill White*, Alex Brinded**
* *past winners of the Sturgeon Cup*

ARTHUR STURGEON CUP

Presented by: Subscribing Members of the Club in 1934

Description: One of the Club's most handsome trophies. In solid silver, it stands 23 inches high, excluding its wooden plinth on which past winners' names are inscribed. It has a circular base of about 7½ inches diameter, with a column and four curved struts supporting a 9 inch diameter globe. Mounted on top of the lid of the globe is a 3 inch high silver figure of a golfer in plus-fours just completing his swing.

Competition: 18 holes, Medal play, competed for annually by the Captain and past Captains.

Winners

1934	T. C. Price	1962	C. G. Williams
1935	A. J. Sturgeon	1963	H. A. Denney
1936	S. H. Titford	1964	W. R. Hall
1937	S. L. Archbutt	1965	L. S. Ellis
1938	S. L. Archbutt	1966	W. R. Hall
1939	S. J. Holford	1967	A. Brinded
1940	C. W. Daborn	1968	S. H. Hewson
1941	N. Y. Marriott	1969	W. R. Hall
1942	S. L. Archbutt	1970	J. M. Davie
1943	W. C. Hindson	1971	W. J. Porter
1944	T. C. Price	1972	J. M. Davie
1945	J. M. Davie	1973	P. F. C. Weeks
1946	G. D. Rosser	1974	G. S. Mallinson
1947	W. C. Hindson	1975	R. H. Avis & G. S. Mallinson*
1948	C. Cunningham	1976	P. F. C. Weeks
1949	S. H. Titford	1977	W. A. Randall & W. J. Porter*
1950	J. M. Davie	1978	W. J. Porter
1951	S. Camm & H. A. Denney*	1979	W. A. Randall
1952	L. Mason	1980	Dr. J. W. T. Pretsell
1953	W. H. White	1981	R. W. Martin
1954	H. A. Denney	1982	W. J. Porter
1955	N. Maclean	1983	G. S. Mallinson
1956	Sir Sydney Camm	1984	W. A. Randall & R. H. Avis*
1957	R. D. Ross	1985	W. A. Randall
1958	A. Brinded	1986	P. H. Thurley
1959	C. Cunningham		
1960	W. H. White		
1961	C. Cunningham		

* Tied

THE VICTORY CUP

Presented by: This is probably the Club's oldest surviving trophy. It is inscribed 'Challenge Bowl' and 'Presented by Captain C. F. Nesham' who was not a Captain of Surbiton but an officer in the armed forces and a Club member in the 1890s. Subsequently, the following inscription was added: 'Re-presented by J. Arnold Hill Esq. as the Victory Cup 1945'. As the name implies, this competition commemorates the Allied victory of the last war.

Description: A solid silver bowl of some 9 inches in diameter, about 5 inches in height, with a circular base and two handles.

Competition: Singles Scratch qualifying round of 18 holes. Best eight scratch scores qualify for Match play. 36 hole final.

Winners

1946	W. J. Kitto	1967	B. T. Wernham
1947	C. S. Walker	1968	B. T. Wernham
1948	W. J. Kitto	1969	F. Clements
1949	W. J. Kitto	1970	A. J. Cook
1950	J. M. Davie	1971	D. L. Hyde
1951	R. W. Greenish	1972	D. L. Hyde
1952	R. W. Greenish	1973	D. L. Hyde
1953	R. W. Greenish	1974	D. L. Hyde
1954	R. S. Hopper	1975	D. Brant
1955	R. S. Hopper	1976	D. L. Hyde
1956	J. M. Davie	1977	A. G. Hutson
1957	R. W. Greenish	1978	A. G. Hutson
1958	R. W. Greenish	1979	A. G. Hutson
1959	G. S. Mallinson	1980	B. T. Wernham
1960	R. W. Greenish	1981	R. M. Sandford
1961	L. W. Welland	1982	N. J. Pimm
1962	L. W. Welland	1983	S. J.Decker
1963	B. T. Wernham	1984	M. C. Nicholls
1964	B. T. Wernham	1985	N. J. Pimm
1965	J. Hutchinson	1986	N. J. Pimm
1966	D. H. Squires		

WINTER FOURSOMES
(also known as The Coleman Cup)

Presented by: Laurence Ide in 1952

Description: Two identical silver cups of traditional design which together with their lids are 8 inches in height and 4¾ inches in diameter. Each cup has two handles and is engraved:

Surbiton Golf Club
The Coleman Cup
Presented by L. H. Ide
1952

Competition: Foursomes Match play knock-out over 18 holes under a handicap limit of 20 with a 36 hole final. Competitors pick their own partners or are drawn on alternate years.

Winners

Year	Winners	Year	Winners
1947	C. Cunningham & T. A. W. Rouse	1961	H. L. Moore & C. H. Lees
1948	J. M. Davie & C. S. Walker	1962	J. P. H. Black & C. H. Lees
1949	J. M. Davie & C. S. Walker	1963	L. W. Welland & W. A. Randall
1950	C. Cunningham & T. A. W. Rouse	1964	D. H. Squires & C. N. Hurst
1951	C. T. Williams & W. J. Mitchell	1965	W. J. Porter & V. A. Dagley
1952	R. S. Hopper & W. A. L. Griffiths	1966	B. T. Wernham & E. S. Lovegrove
1953	C. F. Hurlock & N. J. Nash	1967	E. S. Lovegrove & A. J. Cook
1954	P. Lovatt & A. E. Roux	1968	W. F. Holmes & R. J. Hacon
1955	A. A. Cowie & F. Murray	1969	D. C. Davey & C. B. Mills
1956	R. W. Greenish & J. H. Spurr	1970	W. F. Holmes & W. B. Lewis
1957	C. G. Williams & R. D. Ross	1971	B. T. Wernham & P. S. Plunkett
1958	R. S. Hopper & F. C. Wilson	1972	G. S. Mallinson & A. J. Mallinson
1959	W. P. Beer & P. J. Whitehorn	1973	L. Langford & B. L. Dexter
1960	W. Dogherty & L. Lawrence	1974	A. L. Hunter & P. J. T. Webb

1975	T. E. Long & B. R. Pettitt	1981	P. J. Sullivan & J. R. Gandar
1976	E. J. Warhurst & D. B. Newman	1982	J. A. H. Ayris & H. D. G. Clements
1977	R. E. Baker & D. W. Richardson	1983	P. O'Connell & J. M. Clews
1978	D. T. Blanchard & M. L. Green	1984	D. M. Downing & D. G. Millar
1979	D. H. Squires & N. J. Duffell	1985	N. J. Pimm & H. E. S. Francis
1980	R. M. Sandford & L. G. Rutherford	1986	D. S. Morgan & D. R. C. Munro

VETERANS' CUP

Presented by: D. E. J. Smith and A. Brinded

Description: A solid silver bowl measuring 6 inches in height and 9 inches in diameter, excluding its two handles. Winners' names are inscribed on the trophy which is also engraved with the words:

Surbiton Golf Club
Veterans' Cup
Presented by
Duncan E. J. Smith Esq. and Alex Brinded Esq.
1954

Competition: The qualifying age is 60 years for this Match play, 18 hole competition with full difference of handicap allowed.

1954	A. L. Albright	1971	A. G. Hillier
1955	A. L. Albright	1972	H. W. Weeks
1956	D. E. F. Alexander	1973	F. Poynter
1957	H. A. Denney	1974	C. E. Capp
1958	P. J. Whitehorn	1975	A. E. Weston
1959	D. E. J. Smith	1976	F. W. Austin
1960	E. C. Benson	1977	J. F. Norrie
1961	D. E. J. Smith	1978	F. W. Austin
1962	D. E. J. Smith	1979	M. R. Foulds
1963	A. Brinded	1980	K. R. Barber
1964	C. G. Williams	1981	N. P. Williams
1965	C. G. Williams	1982	H. W. Weeks
1966	P. J. Whitehorn	1983	J. Denyer
1967	L. P. Lawrence	1984	W. H. G. Kinnock
1968	A. L. Salmon	1985	W. F. Holmes
1969	D. G. Kirk	1986	N. R. Griffiths
1970	L. P. Lawrence		

THE CELEBRATION CUPS

Presented by: F. E. Pyrke to celebrate the purchase of the Club in 1957

Description: A solid silver chalice-shaped trophy of about 9½ inches in height and 5 inches in diameter, excluding its two handles. Winners' names are engraved on it as also are the words:

Surbiton Golf Club
1957
The "Celebration" Cup
Presented by
F. E. Pyrke Esq.

Competition: Mixed foursomes, Match play under handicap with handicap limits of 18 (increased to 20 in 1986) for men and 30 for ladies; 18 hole final.

Winners

1958	Mrs. A. J. Albright & Sir Sydney Camm, C.B.E.
1959	Mrs. G. B. L. Ellis & S. R. Wood
1960	Dr. Eiloart & B. DeVetta
1961	Mrs. A. M. Rosser & L. S. Ellis
1962	Mrs. D. Humphrey & Sir Sydney Camm, C.B.E.
1963	Mrs. L. W. Adams and H. B. Fleming
1964	Mrs. J. Brewis and C. G. Williams
1965	Mrs. L. M. Finch & D. C. Davey
1966	Mrs. P. H. Thurley & W. F. Holmes
1967	Mrs. M. Laskey & K. P. Gee
1968	Lady A. M. Newton & C. B. Mills
1969	Mrs. V. Jessup & D. C. Matthews
1970	Mrs. R. W. Martin & L. W. Welland
1971	Mrs. E. K. Leggett & G. Milne
1972	Mrs. B. W. Brady & A. N. Seagrim
1973	Mrs. C. B. Mills & C. Gledhill
1974	Mrs. E. M. Seagrim & L. A. Langford
1975	Mrs. W. B. Lewis & M. J. Prince
1976	Mrs. E. R. Burley & G. H. Pegler
1977	Mrs. J. Hall & B. Wernham
1978	Mrs. M. Seagrim & I. Williams
1979	Mrs. E. R. Burley & B. Wernham
1980	Mrs. E. R. Jenkins & D. G. Millar
1981	Mrs. J. Rubinstein & G. M. Clark
1982	Mrs. J. E. Hall & A. G. E. Stackwood
1983	Mrs. A. D. Cartwright & B. J. Hauldren
1984	Mrs. J. Neal-Smith & P. M. O'Connell
1985	Mrs. M. E. Aulds & Dr. G. M. Clark
1986	Mrs. R. Jenkins & F. I. Valentine

THE EVANS TROPHY

Presented by: The Apostles Golfing Society in 1961 in recognition of the services that Bob Evans had rendered to the Club and to this Society.

Description: A traditional shaped silver cup which, complete with its lid, is 14 inches high. The diameter of the bowl is 6 inches, while that of the circular base is 5½ inches. There are two handles fixed to the lip and base of the bowl.

Competition: Singles Stableford over 18 holes off Medal tees with a maximum handicap of 20 and an allowance of ⅞ths.

Winners

1962	S. H. Hewson	1974	R. G. Fletcher
1963	L. W. Welland	1975	C. O. Clark
1964	P. J. Goodall	1976	I. R. Gillhespy
1965	S. H. Brain	1977	F. W. Girling
1966	D. Harrison	1978	N. Pimm
1967	L. C. Turner	1979	B. C. Munro
1968	D. H. Squires	1980	M. C. Nicholls
1969	K. J. Winton	1981	M. J. Prince
1970	A. M. Stockton	1982	A. W. Tuvey
1971	R. Cain	1983	E. Button
1972	I. R. Gillhespy	1984	H. D. G. Clements
1973	A. G. Hutson	1985	J. T. Tink
		1986	I. MacKay

ROBERT GREENISH CUP

Presented by: Robert Greenish's widow in memory of her husband who was one of the Club's best post-war golfers.

Description: An unembelished solid silver goblet, approximately 8 inches in height and 5 inches in diameter with a curved handle on either side.

Competition: 36 holes of stroke play (scratch).

Winners

1962	B. T. Wernham	1968	A. J. Cook
1963	B. T. Wernham	1969	A. J. Cook
1964	L. W. Welland	1970	D. H. Squires
1965	D. H. Squires	1971	A. J. Cook
1966	D. H. Squires	1972	A. M. Stockton
1967	A. J. Cook	1973	D. T. Blanchard

1974	D. L. Hyde	1981	R. M. Sandford
1975	D. L. Hyde	1982	N. J. Pimm
1976	D. L. Hyde	1983	N. J. Pimm
1977	J. P. Latham	1984	N. J. Pimm
1978	A. G. Hutson	1985	N. J. Pimm
1979	N. J. Pimm	1986	R. M. Sandford
1980	J. L. Larcombe		

THE STEWART HEWSON HOLE IN ONE TROPHY

This trophy, a silver salver, was presented to the Club by Mrs. Cecily Hewson, in memory of her husband (Captain 1967), in 1971. The following names are recorded on the trophy itself, and on small overflow silver plaques in its display case. It is clear from the claims made by some members that the names entered for this trophy do not represent the totality of holes in one achieved by Club members since 1971.

W. F. Holmes	13th	25.11.71
J. H. Flew	17th	27.12.71
E. S. Middleton	13th	9.1.72
V. J. Reynolds	15th	4.4.72
L. A. Langford	11th	7.5.72
G. S. Mallinson	11th	6.6.72
A. A. Cowie	13th	10.6.72
F. W. Girling	13th	6.8.72
A. H. Cree	4th	19.8.72
C. A. F. Jones	4th	20.8.72
L. A. Langford	13th	3.9.72
E. J. Warhurst	11th	15.10.72
N. R. Griffiths	15th	16.12.72
F. W. Austin	13th	13.1.73
D. L. Hyde	15th	3.2.73
F. C. Waller	15th	25.2.73
H. W. Weeks	15th	11.4.73
L. A. Langford	11th	28.5.73
W. J. da Costa	11th	29.5.73
R. R. Langrish	13th	14.7.73
A. H. Mallinson	4th	4.8.73
T. W. Blackmore	11th	29.8.73
R. J. Burgess	13th	24.10.73
C. Gledhill	15th	31.1.74
A. L. Salmon	11th	26.3.74
D. H. Squires	13th	11.5.74
A. Hutson	15th	18.5.74
G. Whitmarsh	13th	13.6.74
L. Perry	13th	15.6.74
W. Kinnock	13th	16.6.74
J. H. Flew	11th	22.6.74
F. Astill	13th	4.7.74
J. J. Frost	15th	19.7.74
J. Hutchinson	13th	25.8.74
C. B. Mills	13th	26.10.74
R. H. Goulsbra	4th	31.7.77
F. C. Knight	11th	23.8.77
A. G. E. Stackwood	15th	17.10.77
S. C. Langford	11th	30.10.77
E. Borrelli	13th	27.1.78
A. G. E. Stackwood	11th	11.3.78
K. W. Hempstead	15th	12.3.79
J. G. Scott	11th	24.3.79
A. W. Colle	4th	5.4.79
C. E. Capp	4th	13.7.79
D. Gillhespy	4th	22.7.79
P. J. T. Webb	13th	22.8.79
J. Larcombe	13th	9.9.79
C. F. Barker	13th	9.9.79
R. E. Baker	11th	6.3.80
P. H. Thruley	4th	18.6.80
M. Green	13th	22.6.80
J. Spurdle	13th	31.8.80
P. A. Browne	13th	26.10.80
J. Williams	15th	31.1.81
N. Spearing	4th	4.4.81
J. Rae	11th	4.4.81
P. Bloxham	4th	9.4.81
C. D. Lloyd	13th	10.5.81
R. W. Davies	13th	14.6.81
K. R. Baker	4th	24.6.81
F. W. Austin	4th	27.3.82
W. H. Jenkins	13th	28.3.82
J. M. Rae	13th	21.8.82
C. B. Williams	15th	28.8.82
J. F. Norrie	13th	18.9.82
F. G. Snell	13th	27.9.82
G. A. Millson	15th	7.1.83
J. R. Denton	13th	8.1.83
D. T. Blanchard	13th	8.1.83

N. R. Griffiths	15th	1.1.75	P. G. Smith	13th	6.2.83
E. S. Minto	13th	27.4.75	K. F. Bantin	4th	13.7.83
A. Green	4th	26.5.75	C. M. Lee	4th	20.7.83
N. J. Brown	13th	28.6.75	D. T. Blanchard	17th	18.4.84
L. G. Rutherford	15th	15.2.76	D. S. Morgan	4th	28.5.84
R. F. Wilson	13th	10.4.76	J. T. Humphries	4th	12.8.84
C. T. Bourne	15th	10.4.76	J. R. Bowman	11th	3.9.84
N. Duffell	4th	11.4.76	N. M. Barnes	11th	25.11.84
F. J. Edmondson	13th	12.4.76	S. Mitchell	11th	27.12.84
P. F. C. Lancaster	13th	19.4.76	L. R. Haskett	4th	7.2.85
A. G. E. Stackwood	15th	3.9.76	K. J. Saunders	17th	24.3.85
F. J. T. Pyrke	13th	29.1.77	J. H. Flew	15th	31.3.85
W. R. Pack	11th	29.1.77	J. M. Ryan	4th	30.4.85
J. Gowers	15th	6.2.77	P. N. Donne-Davis	15th	4.5.85
C. R. Parsley	13th	5.3.77	R. H. Payne	13th	27.5.85
W. C. Barrett	13th	19.3.77	C. Frost	13th	29.7.85
H. S. Howat	13th	29.3.77	G. L. Larcombe	15th	25.8.85
R. D. Kinnersley	11th	25.5.77	K. J. Saunders	11th	8.9.85
K. E. Tomline	11th	7.6.77	H. E. Green	13th	30.11.85
A. D. Thomson	13th	25.6.77	G. A. Huard	11th	18.12.85

SUMMER COMPETITION
(also known as the Summer Cup)

Presented by: The Club in 1979

Description: A 12 inch diameter silver salver which is inscribed on its face:

Surbiton Golf Club
Summer Competition

Winners' names are inscribed on the underside of the salver.

Competition: Four-ball, better-ball, Match play, knock-out under handicap with a limit of 20 and with a 36 hole final.

Winners

1979	R. M. Sandford & G. W. J. Hoskin
1980	W. Bruce & M. Bice
1981	M. Nicholls & P. G. Smith
1982	H. D. G. Clements & J. A. H. Ayris
1983	D. Wordsworth & R. Fletcher
1984	A. P. Stephenson & J. Eastman
1985	Dr. G. M. Clark & D. E. Gillhespy
1986	M. K. Webster & A. H. Cree

CHAPTER 10

THE AMATEUR CHAMPIONSHIP

The Amateur Championship, as the name implies, is regarded as being the premier competition for amateur golfers in Britain. The first official year of the championship was 1886, it having been inaugurated after the success of the 1885 meeting at Hoylake organised by the Royal Liverpool Club.

The handicap limit for entrants is two, it is a Match play competition, with entries limited in more recent years to about 300. The final is played over 36 holes, and the preceding rounds over 18.

Sir Alfred S. Mays-Smith

The first member of Surbiton to play in The Amateur Championship was Alfred Mays-Smith, who was a founder member of the Club and Captain of it in 1900, 1909 and 1920; he lived at 3 Oak Hill, Surbiton. His first attempt was in 1911 at Prestwick when he received a bye in the first round, and then lost to J. H. Andrew of Prestwick in the second. His second attempt the following year at Westward Ho! was no more successful. Again he received a bye in the first round and lost in the second to C. Bell, a member of the home club. In 1913 at St. Andrews, he received a bye for the third time. This time he beat C. Campbell of Tantallon by one hole in the second round, but lost by 5 and 4 in the third to J. R. Beckett of West Kilbride. In Mays-Smith's fourth and last entry in 1914, he was knocked out in the first round by 2 and 1 by C. K. Hutchinson who was a member of the home club and runner up in 1909.

B. Smith

Smith also represented the Club in the 1914 championship at Sandwich, losing in the first round to F. W. H. Weaver of Royal Liverpool by 4 and 3.

R. G. Inglis

As far as is known, no Surbiton members participated in The Amateur again until 1939 when Ronnie Inglis, whose father George was Captain in 1939 and 1940, reached the last 32 at Hoylake. In the first round he beat J. Walker of Coombe Hill at the 19th, in the second he defeated

J. McInnes of Parkstone by one hole, and C. P. Johnstone of India in the third by 2 and 1. In the fourth round he was knocked out by James Bruen of Cork, who won the championship in 1946, by a margin of 4 and 3.

Ronnie Inglis was also Scottish Boys' Champion in 1937 and 1938 winning at North Berwick on each occasion by one hole. Tragically, Ronnie lost his life in the first big bombing raid over Berlin during the last war.

Sir Alfred Mays-Smith
Captain 1900, 1909 & 1920

D. L. Hyde

It was another 34 years before Surbiton was represented again in this championship. Our representative on that occasion, 1973 at Royal Porthcawl, was David Hyde who received a bye in the first round. He then lost in the second by 5 and 4 to M. H. Lygate of Troon Portland. Unless someone has escaped by researches, Hyde was Surbiton's last entry. Do we have to wait another 30 years or so before the challenge is taken up again?

Hyde was arguably Surbiton's finest non-professional player in post-war years: he is no longer a member. His club successes included winning the Robert Greenish Cup three times, in 1974, 1975 and 1976; the Captain's Prize in 1971; the Bradbury Cup in 1974; the Waffrons Cup in 1974 and 1976, and the Victory Cup in 1971, 1972, 1973, 1974 and 1976: he also holds the members' lowest recorded gross score with a round of 64 in a Monthly Medal competition on 5th June, 1976. The course was then 6,211 yards as it is now (1986). His card read as follows:

Hole	*Yards*	*Par*	*Score*	*Hole*	*Yards*	*Par*	*Score*
1	400	4	3	10	380	4	4
2	315	4	3	11	170	3	3
3	418	4	4	12	530	5	4
4	188	3	3	13	125	3	2
5	395	4	4	14	512	5	4
6	385	4	3	15	155	3	4
7	360	4	4	16	443	4	4
8	415	4	3	17	290	4	4
9	280	4	4	18	450	4	4
Out	3156	35	31	In	3055	35	33
				Out	3156	35	31
				Total	6211	70	64
				H'cap			1
				Net Score			63

Hyde was also runner-up in the Golf Illustrated's Gold Vase Match play competition at Walton Heath in May 1976. He scored a one over par 73 on the New course in the first round, added a brilliant 69 over the more difficult Old course in the afternoon, and looked to be the likely winner. It was only an amazing run of five under par for four holes over the last nine to score 32 that gave Allan Brodie of Balmore G.C. a one stroke victory over Hyde.

In the following year, Hyde tried his luck on the professional circuit, with Surbiton G.C. as his attachment, but he did not prosper and gave up after a couple of years.

There have been, of course, a number of other very fine golfers at Surbiton over the years of which R. Large in the early 1900s may have been the best. Other names such as Basil Kemsley, Wally Kitto, Robert Greenish, who held the course record for many years before it was taken from him by Bryan Wernham, who subsequently lost it to

Hyde, are just a few that come to mind, while no-one would dispute that the Club's current best amateur player is Nigel Pimm (1/2 handicap). It is doubtful if anyone will now ever equal or beat Hyde's record 64 as the course has been made more difficult to play since the 1970s, but you never know as illustrated by this story which has nothing to do with The Amateur Championship or the course record.

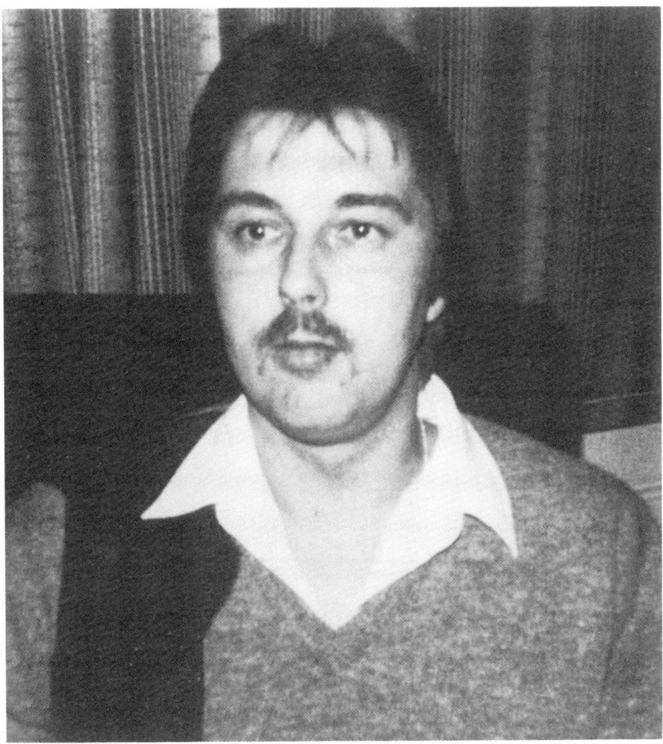

David Hyde
Holder of the Club's current record amateur score

Some years ago Wernham (1 handicap) was playing a four-ball at Surbiton and sank his second shot on the 8th for an eagle 2. As he walked off the green having thought he had won the hole, one of his opponents, Dick Bryant, short of the green, shouted 'Hey I've got this for a half, I get a shot'. Bryant then proceeded to sink his third shot for a net two and a half. The moral of the story is, I suppose, that golf is unpredictable and a game is never won nor lost until the last shot is played – Hyde's record score may yet be bettered!

CHAPTER 11

SURBITON'S PROFESSIONALS

The job of a club professional is by no means a sinecure. While it is usually taken for granted that club professionals are accomplished players of scratch standard, this is not always the case in practice. However, assuming the professional is a quality player, this alone is not enough; he is also expected to be a good teacher, and this particular talent does not necessarily follow automatically from the first. Moreover, in order to survive in this day and age, he has to be able to run a good shop, and to offer sound advice and the right equipment for sale at competitive prices in order to make a decent living. He must also have a thorough knowledge and understanding of the Rules of Golf, know a fair bit about course management and layout, and be able to handle 'difficult' members of both sexes with tact, patience and courtesy. Repairing and maintaining members' golf equipment is another skill that all professionals are expected to possess.

This is quite a portfolio of skills and expertise, which coupled with long hours in the summer months, places quite a demand on any professional. Finally, in order to keep his knowledge and playing skill up to standard, he needs to meet and play with his peers fairly regularly, in addition to all the other demands placed on his time. Nevertheless, a pros' life today is not as arduous and boring as it was in pre-war years, as will be become apparent in a moment.

Surbiton has been fortunate, it would seem, in that most of the professionals (and assistants) it has engaged have fulfilled most of these requirements most of the time. Unfortunately, the background and playing performances of some of the Club's past pros are rather sparsely recorded or no longer exist; apologies may therefore be due to some of our past professionals who perforce have received rather scant and less than fair treatment in this account. In contradistinction, our most famous assistant, Dai Rees, wrote a book about his golfing life, part of which was spent at Surbiton. His book contains some illuminating recollections of the day-to-day life of a professional in the 1930s; these have been extracted and are quoted later in this chapter.

W. Buckle and G. Founds

Surbiton's first professional (and greenkeeper) was W. Buckle. That much is recorded in various journals of the day, i.e. of 1895 and 1896, but little else. He was succeeded in 1897 by George Founds before he in turn was replaced by Hepburn in, it is thought, 1900.

In May 1897, Founds played an exhibition match against J. H. Taylor, who was five-times Open Champion (1894, 1895, 1900, 1909, 1913), and the professional of Royal Wimbledon G.C. from 1896 to 1899. The event attracted a crowd of spectators, '*who were rewarded with as fine a display of golf as has ever been witnessed in the neighbourhood of London*', so said the GOLF journal of 7th May, 1897. The GOLF report on the match was as follows:

'Taylor and Founds started their match at half past two. The latter, like the ex-champion, is an old Westward Ho! caddie, but the two met for the first time on an English green. The young local professional was evidently a little nervous in facing a redoubtable golfer like Taylor: and this no doubt mainly accounted for the rather disappointing figure he made during the first part of the round. He drives a long ball from the tee, the swing being full, easy and graceful. He also manipulates the brassey and cleek with considerable dexterity, but lacks precision both in approaching and putting. Weakness on the green was the sole cause of his losing the first three holes, and although as the match proceeded he overcame his nervousness to some extent, he over and over again lost a hole by missing a short putt. When he gains more confidence he will doubtless be a formidable competitor against men in the front rank to-day; and his admirers predict he will give a good account of himself in The Open Championship at no distant date.

Taylor was in splendid form, and rarely played a better game than he did on Saturday. He gave his opponent 3 strokes in the eighteen holes, two rounds being played. At the ninth in the first round the ex-Champion was 3 up. The only noticeable incident up to this point was a bold bid by Taylor for a 3 at the sixth hole. He just missed getting down a long putt from the edge of the green, the ball resting on the lip of the hole. The ninth was pocketed by Founds with a six-yard putt, Taylor missing a comparatively easy putt for a half in 4. The local professional improved a little coming home and managed to halve five of the nine holes; but Taylor increased his lead to 4 at the finish of the round. Scores for the first round were:—

Taylor	- Out	5 3 4 6 5 4 4 3 5 = 39	77
	— In	6 5 4 5 3 4 4 3 4 = 38	
Founds	- Out	6 4 6 5 6 5 5 3 4 = 44	86
	— In	5 5 6 5 3 4 5 5 4 = 42	

The second round was entered upon after a few minutes' interval. The first hole was indifferently played on both sides. Taylor, singular to relate, foozled his approach shot, which resulted in Founds snatching a half in 6. The second – a thoroughly sporting hole – was halved in 3, perfect play. The next two were also halved in 4 and 5 respectively. At the fifth, Founds with an allowance of a stroke, was enabled to put another half to his credit; but the next was captured by Taylor in 4 against 5.

From the seventh tee, the ex-Champion drove out of bounds into the field to the right, losing stroke and distance, and giving his opponent the hole with a good 4. Founds succeeded in capturing the next also with a perfectly played 3, Taylor taking one more. At the ninth the local man had hard luck, coming into collision with the trees in approaching, and losing a couple of strokes. Taylor won the hole in 4 against 6, making him 4 up at the turn.

Coming home, the ex-Champion got into trouble, driving into a bunker and taking 6 to hole, Founds getting down in 4. A half followed, and at the twelfth Taylor created a flutter of excitement by narrowly escaping holing out in 2. He had a beautiful ten-yard putt, but the ball just rested provokingly on the lip of the hole. As it was he got down in 3, against 4, making him 4 up. Taking the next, he was dormy 5; and the fourteenth being halved, the match finished in favour of Taylor by 5 up and 4 to play. Scores for the second round were:

Taylor	– Out	6 3 4 5 4 4 7 4 4 = 41	79
	— In	6 5 3 4 4 5 3 4 4 = 38	
Founds	– Out	6 3 4 5 5 5 4 3 6 = 41	81
	— In	4 5 4 5 4 4 4 5 5 = 40	

In the bye Taylor was 2 up. Mr. Bulmer Howell, Captain of the Club, acted as umpire; and all the arrangements were effectively carried out under the supervision of Mr. A. H. Lisner, the Hon. Secretary.'

All in all it was a pretty good showing by Surbiton's young pro against one of the finest golfers of the day. Incidentally, at that time George Founds held the Club's record with a gross score of 75. What became of him after he left Surbiton is not recorded.

James Hepburn

From the limited evidence available it is most probable, but not absolutely certain, that James Hepburn was the Club's third professional. The evidence for this is to be found in the list of finishers of The Open where J. Hepburn of Surbiton (his club attachment, not where he lived) is recorded as tying for 33rd place at St. Andrews in 1900 when he scored 351 (89, 86, 87, 89), 42 shots behind the winner, J. H. Taylor.

Hepburn was born and brought up in Scotland where he learnt his golfing skills under Bob Simpson at Carnoustie in the 1890s. With the explosion of interest in golf around this time, and the establishment of many new clubs in the Home Counties and elsewhere, Hepburn came south to become the professional at Enfield, Middlesex. It was while he was at Enfield that he first competed in The Open. This was in 1897 when he tied for 49th place at Hoylake, scoring 365 (97, 93, 91, 84), 51 shots more than Harold Hilton, the winner. There are no records of Hepburn finishing in The Open in 1898 and 1899, although he probably competed, and hence it is not known whether he was by then attached to Surbiton or still with Enfield for one or both of these years.

Further confusion arises from the fact that in the years following 1900, James Hepburn is recorded by the Royal and Ancient in its listings of The Open finishers as being attached to Surbiton in 1903, 1904, 1906 and 1911, to Home Park in 1905, 1907, 1909, 1910 and 1914, and to Hampton Court (another name for Home Park?) in 1908. There are various possible explanations for this apparent frequent change of attachment during this period, the most likely explanation being that it was not uncommon in those days for a professional to be attached to more than one club. Surbiton had a total membership of less than 150 just before the turn of the century, so perhaps the duties of a tournament professional, assuming he had the support of good assistants, were not too onerous and enabled him to divide his time between two adjacent clubs so as to boost his meagre earnings.

Of the twelve times that Hepburn is recorded as a finisher in The Open between 1897 and 1914, his best performance was at the Royal Cinque Ports, Deal, in 1909 when he tied for eighth place, 12 shots behind the winner, J. H. Taylor, who scored 295. This was the first and only time that Hepburn managed to break 80 in all four rounds (78, 77, 76, 76 = 307), and this placed him ahead of such luminaries as Ben Sayers, Tom Vardon, George Duncan, Harry Vardon and Arnaud Massey, all of whom, except Sayers, won The Open in their time. These scores may not seem very impressive by modern-day standards, but it should be remembered that between 1892, when four rounds were introduced for the first time, and 1925, only seven Opens were won with aggregate scores of less than 300, the lowest being James Baird with 291 at Prestwick in 1908. But for most of this period we are talking about hickory-shafted clubs, and quite different balls (gutta-percha) and course conditions than today. And if this wasn't enough, golfers were obliged to play in heavyweight, buttoned-up jackets and collars and ties; surely their clothing alone, apart from the quality of their equipment, must have inhibited their play to some extent, or so one would think. On the other hand, Harry Vardon, one of the greatest golfers of all time, and six-times winner of The Open (1896, 1898, 1899, 1903, 1911, 1914), said in his book of tips for beginners in 1905:

'*Always use braces in preference to a belt round the waist. I never play with a belt. Braces seem to hold the shoulders together as they ought to be. When a man plays in a belt he has an unaccustomed sense of looseness and his shoulders are too much beyond control. For the same reason, I do not advise a golfer to play without his coat, even on the warmest day, if he wants to play his best game*'.

Perhaps he had a point as the best hole I have personally ever played at Surbiton was an eagle-3, instead of my usual double-bogey, on the twelfth (a driver, a 5-wood and one putt) when wearing two thick constricting sweaters and waterproof over-trousers, but no braces! Be that as it may, no Surbiton professional featured again in The Open until over 20 years later when Dai Rees finished 19 shots behind Alfred Perry of Leatherhead at Muirfield in 1935.

Two other notable achievements of Hepburn were when he lost in the semi-finals of the PGA Match Play Championship to J. H. Taylor at Mid-Surrey in 1904, and again in the semi-finals to Sandy Herd at Walton Heath in 1909. Hepburn also represented Scotland against England, then the only form of representative golf, in 1903, 1905, 1906, 1907, 1909, 1910, 1912 and 1913.

All in all he was quite a player of his time, not quite a Dai Rees perhaps, but very good for all that. In 1913 or 1914 Hepburn left Surbiton, and in 1918 he went to live in the United States where for 20 years he was the pro at the National Golf Links, Southampton, New York, in the summer, and at the Mid-Ocean Club, Bermuda, during the winter, continuing, it would seem, his dual club attachment arrangement that he had had with Surbiton and Home Park before the first World War. It is not known what Hepburn's playing record was whilst he was living in North America.

Hepburn's ability to compete regularly in The Open, the PGA, and his frequent appearances for Scotland, prove that he was a professional of high quality; Surbiton can be proud to have had such a professional attached to it during the Club's early years.

James Coleman

Surely Jim Coleman, as he was usually called, must be almost unique in professional golfing circles if only in regard to the length of time, fifty years, that he spent with one club – longer if one includes his time as an assistant. Surprisingly, for someone with such a long and prominent association with the Club, little factual material now exists on Jim Coleman as far as his playing record is concerned. Fortunately, as it so happens, he is mentioned a number of times in Dai Rees's book, thus much of what there is to recount about Coleman actually appears in the following section under Rees.

Coleman was born in Kent on 2nd January, 1890. Where, and under whose guidance, he learnt the game is not known. Circumstantial evidence suggests that Coleman joined the staff of Surbiton some years before 1912, presumably as what we now term an 'assistant', although it may not have been quite so formal an appointment in those days as it now tends to be. It would then appear he succeeded to the position of club professional when Hepburn concluded his attachment with Surbiton shortly before the outbreak of the Great War. From then on, until he retired on 1st July, 1962, at the age of 72, he served continuously as Surbiton's professional.

Dai Rees and Jim Coleman

In his latter years, according to the recollections of some of our older members, Coleman did not play very often himself. Regular games with the Captain and other members were not then quite such a feature of the Club's activities as they have become in more recent years. And, of course, he was helped in his duties both on and off the course by such good assistants as, for example, Dai Rees, Billy Hotten, his son-in-law, and Peter Gill.

By all accounts, Coleman was no mean player in his younger days, but I have not been able to unearth what his playing record may have been, if in fact he ever entered into the wider arena of national professional competitions. He must also have been held in high regard by many of his more famous contemporaries as during the 1920s and 1930s, world renowned players such as The Open winners James Braid (Open winner 1901, 1905, 1906, 1908 and 1910), Ted Ray (1912) and Arthur Havers (1923), came and played with Jim Coleman at Surbiton.

But playing records, whatever they may be, are but one measure of a professional. More important, at least as far as club professionals are concerned, is the regard in which they are held by their members. As far as Jim Coleman is concerned, the following comments taken from letters I have received from some of the Club's senior members speak for themselves:

'I always had a great regard for Jimmie Coleman. I thought him a man of character, very shrewd, and a great judge of men. He must have been held in great respect for he was granted the privilege of the use of the clubhouse. I saw Jimmie play only once; this was in a 'Celebration' fourball (in 1957) including Dai Rees, who came especially for the occasion, and Sir Sydney Camm'.

and

'Outstanding in my memory is Jimmy Coleman, professional, teacher and Father Confessor to us all. He had nothing more than a shed for his shop, but it was to him we went every time our game went wrong, and no matter how often you called on him you received a sympathetic hearing, and, after a fatherly lecture, you came out of his shop, feeling much better'.

and

'He was always ready to help. He always got our (ladies) trolleys out for us. One of Nature's gentlemen'.

and

'Jim would open his shop at about 7.30 a.m. every day and stay open until it was dark, he never seemed to have days off or holidays . . . He carried a drainpipe bag with just a few old clubs and had a very short swing. Many would disparge his style, but few could beat him. A canny player, never off the fairways and red hot around the greens. A wonderful putter, using a curved shafted putter which were subsequently banned by the R & A . . . He is known to have scored at least 15 holes in one at Surbiton . . . Coleman was one of Nature's gentlemen with a wonderful philosophy of life. No rancour or bitterness at the way he was

treated by some members. He was one of the most contented and genuinely happy men I have ever met'.

In fact everyone, it would seem, who was a member when Coleman was the pro, speaks highly of him and with affection. Tangible evidence of the esteem in which he was held was the resolution proposed by Percy Weeks (Captain 1970 and 1971), seconded by W. J. Mitchell, and carried by acclamation at the Club's AGM in June, 1962. It was: '*the General Committee be empowered at their absolute discretion to arrange on behalf of the Club ... a pension or annual payment to Mr. James Coleman to mark the Club's appreciation of his excellent services as Professional extending over the past 50 years*'.

Coleman lived for most of his time at Surbiton in one of the few remaining old cottages (No. 66), where his widow still lives, in nearby Clayton Road. Sadly, Jim Coleman did not survive to enjoy his retirement from the Club for very long; he died on 28th November, 1963, and is buried in St. Paul's churchyard, Hook Road, less than one mile from the Club.

David 'Dai' Rees, C.B.E.

Rees was never the professional at Surbiton, but as assistant to Jim Coleman for some four years over the period 1934–1938, and the most successful and famous golfer ever to be closely associated with the Club, he can hardly be omitted from this account.

Dai Rees, as he was universally known, was born near Barry, Glamorgan, in March 1913, the son of a Welsh professional. His playing record, which I shall come to later, was quite outstanding. He first hit a golf ball on a proper course a few days after his fifth birthday when a member at The Leys, his father's club, thrust a cut-down four-wood into his hands and teed up a ball on a pile of wet sand for him on the 250 yard, par-3, twelfth. Dai was down in four, his fourth shot holing out from sixty yards. Rees turned professional at the age of fifteen and devoted virtually the rest of his life to golf. Let us now turn to Rees's own account of his time at Surbiton which I have extracted from his book 'Thirty Years of Championship Golf' published by Stanley Paul in 1968:

'In July, 1934, a sports goods representative, Andy Duncan, walked into the shop and told me that Mr. James Coleman, the pro at Surbiton, had hinted to him that he wanted an assistant. Without stopping even to write, I left Aberdare immediately, accompanied by the steward, Iowal Davies, a big-hearted man who had been wounded in the leg in the First World War, and we took an express train to Paddington and then a suburban-line train to Surbiton.

As we walked up the hill towards the club we were passed by a tall(?), broad-shouldered man riding a bicycle. It proved to be Mr. Coleman and, after he heard of my enthusiasm in travelling from Wales to join him, he offered me twenty-five shillings a week retainer as his assistant.

The agreement was that I should live at his home and pay one pound each week towards my living expenses. So, as a young Welshman with a strong accent and nothing to recommend me but some slight skill with a golf club, I entered into the routine of a London suburban golf club. It was a curious change from the free-and-easy life at Aberdare. At Surbiton, neither Mr. Coleman nor myself were allowed to mix with the members in the clubhouse and to obtain a drink we had to go round to the back of the bar.

The whole thing was very different from my dreams of fame and prestige. There is much talk about snobbery in golf. Young pros all over the world are striving for recognition as individuals, as indeed are young people in every walk of life. I can say, however, quite honestly, that I did not think of myself at that time as a victim of snobbery. This was the way of life in the South of England and virtually a foreign atmosphere for a Welshman. Perhaps I was unlucky in my choice of a time to move, for the Kingston By-Pass was then being built, largely with Irish and Welsh labour. The Dubliners, and my own countrymen, with their extravagant speech and ability to drink and swear better than the English, were not being received with acclaim.

Mr. Coleman was a man of Kent and a professional of the old school, who never expected me to do anything that he could not, or did not occasionally, do himself. Two hundred sets of clubs, most hickory-shafted and not rustless, were kept in the shed at the back and these had to be cleaned perfectly by rubbing each club individually with emery paper to get the mud and rust off the iron heads.

Late every Saturday night we cleaned the lot, ready for use again on Sunday morning, and on each Sunday night we repeated the process, and cleaned them yet again on a Monday so that they would be ready, either for a casual round during the week or for the following weekend play. Another chore was to collect about one hundred pairs of muddy shoes in sacks to be scrubbed and polished to a state satisfactory to their owners. As I nursed my tired limbs and sore fingers, I thought ruefully that I might have been better off staying in Aberdare.

The early months of 1935 were frustrating ones. As far as the members at Surbiton were concerned, I was a nobody. I was simply a little Welshman who could hit the ball reasonably well but who had apparently no qualifications for teaching them to hit a better ball, and so I gave very few lessons, and I played in only two or three events. One of these was the Assistants' Championship, in which I had been narrowly beaten by Bob Porter the year before. It was played at St. Annes Old, and had reverted to strokeplay, which I felt was a distinct disadvantage to me, and yet I won it by one stroke from Bill Cox, with a total of 284. This victory did me more good at Surbiton than I expected, and my diary of engagements suddenly filled up. To have a lesson, or a round, with 'young Rees' was one thing; to be taught by the British Assistants' Champion was, apparently, quite another.

During that winter I practised very hard and, early in 1936, I managed to finish runner-up in a Guildford Alliance meeting, and won a variety of sweepstake money, which totalled forty-five pounds. I went home loaded with envelopes and, as Mrs. Coleman had not been well, I cheered her up by dancing into the lounge, heaping them all into her lap and announcing: 'There you are ma'am. See what we've won!'.

I was twenty-two and trying hard to consolidate my moderate success. At six each evening, after finishing work in the pro's shop or the clubhouse, I played a 'loop' of holes from the sixth to the ninth, using different clubs for various shots.

I made new friends, too. A family called Inglis arrived from Scotland and they all took up golf with considerable success, especially their young son Ronald. Mr. and Mrs. Inglis treated me as if I were a second son. One day, for example, when I was cycling to a tournament at Roehampton with my clubs slung across my shoulders, I overbalanced and fell heavily. I played the event with a grazed leg and side which stiffened up as the round wore on. Mrs. Inglis promptly decided that, in future, she would drive me to all London tournaments, and she was as good as her word. I will always be grateful for the kindness shown me by this family. It helped an awful lot. Ronald later became Scottish Boys' Champion, etc., but alas! was lost over Hamburg (Berlin?) with the R.A.F.

Mr. Coleman proffered little advice. When he did, it was sound stuff. 'Try to play the ball round in the bogey (i.e. par in today's parlance) of the course. Score consistently in the mid-70s and you'll always be in the money', he said.'

After describing some of his disappointments, including not being selected for the 1935 Ryder Cup team, Rees goes on to say:

'There ensued a grey and depressing period in my life, during which I never quite lost the feeling that I had it in me to break through. I arose every morning at five o'clock and practised for

> two or three hours before running back to one of Mrs. Coleman's huge breakfasts. My game began to assume a solid shape. I had acquired the knack of flicking the ball with my clubs when I was a small boy in Wales and when I was never allowed to hit full shots in case I broke windows. I had to be content with flicking balls twenty or thirty yards on a patch of ground near the clubhouse, and I am convinced that it was this early training that enabled me to develop a hand action that is at the heart of my swing today'.

and

> 'At the time of my development at Surbiton, many people were advising me to change my grip. I used a two-handed grip, that is one with no interlocking of the fingers, and it was strongly suggested to me that I should change, either to the Vardon overlapping grip, or to an interlocking one, similar to that used by Mr. Coleman.'

In 1937, Rees played in the Ryder Cup match at Southport, an automatic choice as he was then the Match Play Champion. He was paired with Charles Whitcombe in the foursomes against Gene Sarazen and Denzil Shute and halved the match. In the singles he was drawn against Byron Nelson and won the match by three and one. He goes on to say:

> 'At Surbiton, I received a big reception after my victory over Nelson, and the publicity I enjoyed for a few short months caused me to receive some offers of interesting jobs. One of these was at the Wilshire Country Club in Los Angeles, California, and I have often wondered how the lives of myself and family would have been changed had I accepted this glamorous appointment. I turned the offer down with thanks. Britain means home to me with a capital H and always will do. The stability, common sense and strong, even old-fashioned, individuality of the people convinced me that it is the best environment in the world.
>
> Although I enjoy travelling, and am basically a nomadic kind of fellow, I could never see myself settling down in another country. After receiving so many offers, however, I became a little unsettled at Surbiton and, upon receiving the opportunity, I moved to Hindhead. This was just before the Second World War. My driving had become inconsistent and Hindhead, which has some of the narrowest fairways in the world, straightened it out.'

I have deliberately quoted from Ress's book at some length as it gives such a good insight on a pros' life between the wars, and more particularly during his time at Surbiton.

There have been very few British golfers as good as or better than Rees. Arguably, he was the best British golfer not to win The Open, although he nearly did so on several occasions. His playing record speaks for itself, the highlights of which are summarised below.

He was runner-up in The Open three times. The first occasion was in 1939, when he tied for second place behind the winner, Dick Burton, at St. Andrews. In 1954, at Birkdale, he tied again, one stroke behind Peter Thomson's winning total of 283. The third occasion was perhaps the most notable as he was then 48 years of age; this was at Royal Birkdale in 1961 when he scored 68, 74, 71, 72 just one shot behind Arnold Palmer. He also came third, after Snead and Cotton, at St. Andrews in 1946, and at Troon in 1950 with rounds of 71, 68, 72 and 71.

Rees was particularly strong at Match play winning the British Professional Match Play Championship in 1936, when he beat Ernest Whitcombe in the final; in 1938 (Eddie Whitcombe); 1949 (Henry Cotton); 1950 (Frank Jowle), and 1967 (Peter Thomson). His successes in the Ryder Cup underline this: he was a Ryder Cup team member in 1937, 1947, 1949, 1951, 1953, 1955 (captain), 1957 (captain), 1959 (captain) and 1961 (captain), as well as being non-playing captain in 1967. 1957, at Lindrick, was the last time prior to 1985 when the Americans did not win.

Some other notable victories during his career were: the British Assistants' Championship at St. Annes Old in 1935 (284), and at Molesey, Birmingham, in 1936 (278); the Irish Open at Portmarnock in 1948 (295); the Belgian Open in 1954; the Swiss Open in 1959 and 1963; the (British) Masters in 1950 and 1962: there were other successes, and many high finishes in various major competitions in the UK and overseas.

In 1957, he received BBC's TV Sportsman of the Year Award, and in 1958 he became a Commander of the British Empire, for services to sport, in the New Year's honours list. He died in 1984 at the age of 71.

Although Dai Rees spent only four years at Surbiton, he continued to visit the Club from time to time and retained a real interest in its affairs, together with a genuine affection for the Colemans.

Peter Gill

Gill joined the staff of the Club as assistant to Jim Coleman in early 1960, having won, like Dai Rees nearly twenty-five years earlier, the Assistant Professionals' Championship the previous year. With the retirement of Coleman in 1962, Peter Gill succeeded him as the Club's professional with a retainer of £312 per annum. By way of comparison, Coleman's retainer a little before Gill joined him as assistant was £208 per annum.

Gill was, and for that matter still is, a fine player. He holds the

Club's course record at 63 off the medal tees, and on one occasion when playing with John Hutchinson, a member, he scored 58 (two 29s) off the yellow tees – most probably another record.

In 1969 he was Surrey Open Champion and Surrey Match Play Champion. In that year he also tied for third place with Neil Coles behind Tony Jacklin and the winner, Christie O'Connor, in the John Player Classic. The first prize of £25,000 was a record itself in those days.

Peter Gill left Surbiton on the best of terms in 1970 to become professional at Gatton Manor G.C. for three years, before moving to his present attachment with Knole Park G.C., Sevenoaks. He still plays at Surbiton from time to time where he continues to be most welcome.

Peter Gill (left) receiving the Wilson Tropy for his victory in the Southern Professional Golfers' Winter league, April 1967

Brian Purdie

Purdie was engaged as professional, with a retainer of £704 per annum, from Falkirk Tryst in 1971 following the amicable resignation of Gill whose move to Gatton Manor was with the intention of spending more time on the professional tournament circuit. Purdie was only with the Club for about a couple of years before he moved to

Blackpool to become the professional at the North Shore municipal club.

J. A. 'Sandy' Meadon

Purdie's replacement, Sandy Meadon, joined the Club in 1973 and stayed for a little over four years. When he left Surbiton he obtained a post as a teaching professional at one of London's large stores. Meadon was one of those professionals whose ability to teach was well recognised and out-matched his own playing performance. Peter Chapman was his assistant.

Paul Milton

The Club's current popular pro, Paul Milton, took up golf as a career when he left school at the age of 15. His first position in 1966 was as an assistant at Coombe Wood, where he got his handicap down from 15 to scratch in a couple of years. From there he went to Banstead Downs, before becoming senior assistant at the well known Moor Park G.C., Richmansworth. While he was at Moor Park, he was also engaged in teaching golf at the famous Harrow School.

Milton, another fine player and a good teacher, was appointed Surbiton's professional in February 1978. During his time with the Club he has won a number of Pro-Am competitions and other events. His more notable successes include:

- South Region PGA Champion, 1981;
- Surrey Open Champion in 1982 at Surbiton, where he tied with David Talbot on 139 after 36 holes, and then won the sudden death play-off on the second hole;
- Harry Secombe Classic Pro-Am 1985;
- Surrey Open runner-up in 1985 at Walton Heath and in 1986 at Hankley Common.

Paul Milton is also Captain of the Croydon and District Alliance, and was Captain of Surrey PGA for the 1982/83 season.

Milton currently has two assistants, John Luff and John Fitzpatrick. Luff, the senior assistant, has been with the Club since 1980, a scratch player, who qualified at the PGA's school with honours. In the Club's 1984 Pro-Am competition on 12th May, Luff scored a hole in one at the 13th and won for himself a £6,500 Vauxhall Cavalier car.

This competition was inaugurated in 1979 and was immediately an unqualified success. Apart from Milton's own efforts in bringing this relatively new annual event to fruition, much of the credit for the overall organisation of each Pro-Am from 1979 until 1982 must go to Committee Member, Peter Webb, who sadly died that year.

To end on a more cheerful note, it is pleasing to record that Paul Milton won the Pro-Am in 1981 with a score of 67, and was joint winner in 1982 with a score of 69, on both occasions against strong opposition from well-known visiting professionals.

Paul Milton with his assistants John Luff and John Fitzgerald

CHAPTER 12

SECRETARIES AND STEWARDS

While the Captain and the Committee are the principal decision takers for most issues of importance, it is the Club Secretary who is required to implement many of the decisions they take, as well as being responsible for ensuring that the day-to-day administration of the Club runs smoothly and effectively. Without the support of an efficient and competent Secretary, some matters the Committee wish to implement may be frustrated, or at least may not turn out quite so well as was originally intended. The Secretary also provides the vital continuity link as Captains and Committee Members come and go. And it is to him that many members turn for guidance and advice, sometimes for instant rulings, on a whole variety of matters some of which may be, strictly speaking, outside his remit. Tact, patience and courtesy are essential requirements of the job, in addition, of course, to the management skills he needs to possess to perform his duties satisfactorily.

All the foregoing is no doubt self-evident, but nevertheless it needs to be stated as all too often good administration is taken for granted, whereas in its absence minor problems can sometimes become magnified out of all proportion. Moreover, although in the past the post of Secretary in many golf clubs, including that at Surbiton from time to time, was often filled on a honorary basis by retired Army or Naval officers, more or less irrespective of whether or not they were skilled in administration and had a good understanding of golfing matters, nowadays the duties and responsibilities of a golf club Secretary have become far more complex to the point where training courses and books are available to instruct and assist them in how to perform their duties. This increasing complexity is reflected, inter alia, by the fact that some clubs have retitled the post, Secretary/Manager, or even General Manager, which better expresses what is now expected of the incumbent.

Unfortunately, it has not been possible to track down every name, and the years concerned, of all those who have served the Club as Secretary, nor for that matter as Steward, prior to the 1930s. Nor is it possible to comment meaningfully on most of those who filled these positions since then, particularly as the tenure of many of them was rather short. However, and leaving to one side the present popular incumbents of these two positions, it would be less than fair not to mention, if only briefly, one or two individuals who are still remembered with kindness and with gratitude for the services they rendered to the Club and its members.

Ernie Newman was a Club member for some years prior to being appointed Secretary by Harry Denney in his year of Captaincy (1950/51). Newman was Secretary for nearly eleven years, until he retired in 1961, and was greatly liked and respected by all. He was small in stature but large in his services to the Club, especially during the difficult days of 1956 and 1957 when the continued existence of the Club hung virtually by a thread. By all accounts he was a great character, very polite and correct, with a whimsical smile, and a great believer in golf club etiquette – woe betide anyone who transgressed the recognised and accepted standards of the day. When Newman retired, the Club not only presented him with a television set and a cheque subscribed by Club members, but on the proposal of Johnnie Baugh and Leslie Ellis, he was unanimously elected at the 1961 AGM an Honorary Member of the Club, an honour rarely conferred on any golf club secretaries. Sadly, Ernie Newman's retirement was all too brief; he died in 1962.

Len Crawforth was another Secretary who was both popular with the members and very efficient in performing his duties, two attributes which are not always easy to combine with success. His administrative qualities were of a particularly high standard, and must have greatly helped the work of the Captains and Committees during the five years he served the Club before he retired in 1970.

Apart from Newman and Crawforth, also Crowne who was Secretary for the best part of twenty years but of whom little is now known, and, of course, the present incumbent, Mike Wright, most other Secretaries during the 1960s and 1970s came and went all too quickly.

This was a worrying and unsettling period for the Club's officers which was not helped by the even more frequent turnover of the Club's Stewards, a trend that was only arrested by the appointment of Arthur and Edna Smith, the present incumbents, in 1979. To some extent, this turnover can be explained partly by the uncertainties that continued to persist, at least in the minds of some of the Stewards in question, even after the Club was purchased in 1957, and also by the fact that there were many more alternative job opportunities in the 1960s and 1970s than have been available in more recent years. But whatever may have been the reasons for these comings and goings in individual cases, and some are perhaps best left unsaid, one should not minimise the part that a good Steward can play in club life, a role that can only be performed effectively with the necessary degree of continuity and commitment.

In concluding this necessarily short chapter, a mention of Frank and Chris Frend, who served the Club so well during those difficult years during and immediately after the war, is appropriate: several of our older members continue to remember them in kindly and affectionate terms. Frank (handicap 2/3) must also have been a mighty smiter of the ball as it is reputed that he once drove the first hole, although it was somewhat shorter then than it is today. Further evidence of his prowess is that he, and some of the long-hitting Club members of this era, used to drive regularly over the trees to the right of the eighteenth tee with a cut-up 4 wood or Spoon (a 3 wood with a shorter shaft) landing the ball way down the right-hand side of the fairway well beyond where the present bell is located. From there all they required to reach the green, for what was then a par-5 hole, was a Niblick (the equivalent of a modern-day 9 iron), or at the most, a Mashie (equivalent to about a 5 iron). Undoubtedly, the trees have grown somewhat since those days, even so I personally have never witnessed nor heard of any member in recent times deliberately aiming to straighten this dogleg by the tree top route! It is, of course, occasionally still done, but more I suspect as a fortuitous act rather than as a deliberate intention. Apologies to any member who may strongly refute this scurrilous observation.

L-R *Ernie Newman (Secretary 1951–1961), Sir Sydney Camm (Captain 1948, 1951 & 1952) and Charles Hurlock (Captain 1954) receiving The Waffrons Challenge Cup in 1951*

How Frank Frend, with his low handicap and self-taught swing, found time to play golf is a mystery in itself. In his day, and presumably during the times of his predecessors as well, the Steward and his wife had a pretty strenuous life. By way of illustration, Frend was required to scrub the stone floors and to clean the men's locker room, bar and toilets at least three times a week, while his wife coped with the lounge, the ladies' rooms and toilets, as well as with all the catering, cooking and serving at table. Between times they served behind the bar, all with no help except on Sunday mornings and at weekend lunchtimes.

How times, and for that matter the needs and habits of members, have changed. Nowadays members expect the bar to be open for long hours every day making this task alone a full-time job for the Steward; certainly the full range of jobs and services now required could not be performed satisfactorily any longer by a couple of people without assistance.

A list – it is incomplete – of all known Club Secretaries and Stewards is given in the Appendix to this chapter.

Mike Wright, Secretary/General Manager since 1977

Arthur Smith, Steward since 1979, his wife Edna and Ron Barham his deputy

SECRETARIES

1895	A. H. Lisner
1896	H. E. Walton
1897–?	H. Wood-Smith & C. H. Evans (joint)
?–1913–?	H. Kidson
*c*1915–*c*1920	W. (Walter) Lucas
1921–?	A. J. Barham
?–1927–?	Lt. Col. E. S. Gillman
*c*1930–*c*1933	Cdr. A. (Arthur) E. Conn, R.N.(ret.)
*c*1933–1951	Capt. C. E. Crowne
1951–1961	T. E. (Ernest) Newman
1961–1963	G. (George) T. Simpson
1963 (5 weeks)	K. A. McKenzie
1963–1966	Lt. Cdr. P. L. S. Baxendale, R.N.(ret.)
1966–1970	L. (Len) J. Crawforth
1970–1972	E. (Eric) Bolton
1973–1975	J. (John) S. F. Woolcock
1976–1977	Major E. (Eric) Lowes, M.C.
1977–	M. (Mike) O. Wright

STEWARDS

1895–*c*1925	?
?–1926–?	Mrs. Proctor
*c*1930–?	Mackenzie
1937–1939	L. G. Emery
1940–?	S. J. Clarke
*c*1940–1957	F. W. Frend
1958	W. Hotton
1959	Goodfellow
1960–1962	Sutton
1963	Fowler
1964	Dickenson
1965	Davidson
1966	Mogford
1967–1971	K. Writtle
1971–1972	Geeson
1973–1974	Forde
1975	M. O. Wright
1976–1979	D. J. Westnutt
1979–	A. Smith

CHAPTER 13

SOME OBSERVATIONS OF A FINANCIAL NATURE

Subscriptions

As one would expect, members' subscriptions have always been the Club's largest single source of annual income. In 1896, the Club's first full year, total income from subscriptions was less than £400. Whereas it took sixty years for the income from subscriptions to increase by a factor of ten, i.e. they amounted to £3,866 in 1956, it took only another twenty-two years for this source of income to increase ten-fold again, i.e. to £39,263 in 1978: by 1985 subs topped the £100,000 mark for the first time.

As far as individual member's subscriptions are concerned, these have risen from 3 guineas for a full gentleman member in 1896, and 1½ guineas for a full lady member, to £231 and £175 respectively in 1985, both exclusive of Value Added Tax which was introduced by the Government of the day in April 1973. Interestingly, if one calculates the effects of inflation and deflation over the years from 1896 to 1985, the equivalent value of 3 guineas (or £3.15) in 1896 was £176 in 1985. Thus one could argue that the actual increases in annual subscriptions over the period 1896 to 1985 have outstripped the effects of inflation/deflation by some £55. However, this simple arithmetic comparison ignores the very real improvements that have been made to the course and clubhouse and to the Club's activities and facilities over the years. While it is impossible to place a value on these improvements in terms of the annual subscriptions now levied, I suspect that few members, if any, would disagree that the 1985 subscription of £231 was most probably better all-round value than the 3 guineas of yesteryears. Come to think of it, there is no member living who can make such a comparison!

Two points worthy of mention are that there were two periods of deflation since the turn of the century, from 1921 to 1923, and from 1926 to 1933 inclusive; this is something we tend to forget after so many years of inflation since the last war. The second is that in earlier years male members were referred to as gentlemen, now simply men – another sign of changing times – whereas ladies, God bless them, are still lady members.

To the extent that records exist, subscriptions for full men and lady members have evolved as follows, with proportionate lower rates for other classes of membership, e.g. 5-day, junior, country, juvenile and social members.

Annual Subscriptions

As at 31st March of the year in question and exclusive of VAT from 1973.

	Full Men	*Full Lady*
1896	£3.3s.0d	£1.11s.6d
1926	£6.6s.0d	£3.3s.0d
1931	£8.8s.0d	£4.4s.0d
1957	£15.15s.0d	£10.10s.0d
1960	£17.12s.6d	£11.15s.0d
1963	£22.10s.0d	£15.0s.0d
1965	£26.5s.0d	£17.10s.0d
1967	£30.00	£20.00
1969	£35.00	£23.00
1971	£42.00	£30.00
1973	£52.00	£38.00
1974	£56.00	£42.00
1975	£66.00	£50.00
1977	£76.00	£58.00
1978	£86.00	£68.00
1979	£120.00	£95.00
1980	£132.00	£104.00
1981	£158.00	£120.00
1982	£174.00	£132.00
1983	£192.00	£146.00
1984	£202.00	£153.50
1985	£216.00	£164.00
1986	£231.00	£175.00
1987	£243.00	£184.50

What effect, if any, increases in subscriptions have had on membership is impossible to assess. Suffice it to say that in most years since the 1960s there has been a substantial waiting list of men wishing to join the Club as full members.

Other Sources of Income

The second largest source of annual income has been the gross profit on the sale of beer, spirits, wine and tobacco. This has risen from £1,555 in 1955, to over £5,000 in 1972, and to nearly £40,000 in 1986. Apart from the undoubted effects of inflation – a double whiskey cost 4 old pennies in the early 1900s – the substantial rise in income in more recent years can be partly attributed to the enlargement and refurbishment of the nineteenth hole bar in 1981; prior to that time the old bar was little more than a large cupboard, or so it seemed! As mentioned elsewhere, the new bar has induced many players to stay for a drink after their game, instead of departing for home or to an outside hostelry, if they were not correctly dressed to use the more formal lounge bar.

The third largest source of income has been green fees. These have risen from £530 in 1955 to top £36,000 in 1986. This has been helped by the boom in golf and the consequential formation of hundreds of golfing societies; there is seldom a week now when the Club does not act as host to several visiting societies. They may, at times, be regarded by some members as a bit of a nuisance by stopping general play for an hour or so while they tee off, but on reflection most members would accept that the income from individual visitors and societies more than compensates for any inconvenience they might cause. To put it another way, if their visits were curtailed, subscriptions would have to be raised.

Next in order of importance is the income from fruit machines. This appears for the first time in the Club's published accounts in 1971 when it amounted to £2,366; by 1986 it was over £14,700.

Last but not least are entrance fees. The first separate record of these fees appears in the 1973 accounts when they represented an income of £876, based on £25 for full men members and £10 for full lady members. However, they were levied for many years prior to the last war, although it appears that they were waived during the war. At the 1972 Annual General Meeting it was proposed by the newly appointed Captain, Alastair Craig, that as from 1st April, 1973, entrance fees should be equivalent to one year's subscription; this resolution was approved unanimously and this basis has applied ever since.

There is in fact one other entry of consequence on the income side of the profit and loss account. Over the years this has been labelled variously 'catering', 'functions and competitions', etc.; it has tended to be a bit of a residue item for a variety of activities. Most years this has been a loss item, but there have been a few occasions when modest profits have been generated.

So leaving aside special one-off fund-raising loans and appeals to members for monies for specific purposes which are dealt with elsewhere in this book, the bedrock of the Club's financial strength has been subscriptions, bar profits and green fees, with income from visiting societies, fruit machines and entrance fees only becoming significant in more recent years.

Expenditure

Traditionally, expenditure items in the Club's accounts have been grouped under three main headings - Upkeep of Course, House Expenses and Other Expenses. As to the first, this usually comprises wages of the ground staff, invariably the largest item, fertilisers, turf, fuel and maintenance of machinery, and in more recent years, water. Over the last thirty years, there are no records remaining for earlier years, the cost of upkeep of the course has risen by a factor of 30, i.e. from about £2,000 in 1955 to just over £60,000 in 1985. For most years course upkeep has represented about one-third of total annual expenditure.

Coincidentally, House Expenses have followed an almost identical pattern, i.e. about £1,800 in 1955 to nearly £57,000 in 1985. This group of expenditure items includes the wages of the house staff, again invariably the largest single item, staff meals, heating and lighting, cleaning and maintenance, laundry, etc.

The third group of expenditure, Other Expenses (more recently termed Administration Expenses), is, of course, the residue of expenditure items. This has increased from £2,000 in 1955 to £53,000 in 1985, i.e. by a factor of 26, not too different from the pattern of other expenditures. The items included in this group include the Secretary's salary (comparison here is less meaningful as in the past it was almost an honorary job, whereas now it also includes secretarial support services), staff accommodation, the professional's retainer, telephone, printing and stationery, insurance, audit and other fees, depreciation and various other expenses. Included in the latter are rates which interestingly have risen by a factor of 13 since 1955, i.e. from £331 to £4,464 (1985).

From the foregoing it will be gathered that Club expenditure has followed, both as to its totality and for most of the items of consequence, a fairly constant and regular pattern: in 1955 total expenditure was £5,735, in 1985 £169,933, almost exactly a thirty-fold increase over the period.

Concluding Comments

The foregoing simple analysis of the income and expenditure accounts is, of course, only one part of the story. Of equal importance are the balance sheets which better portray the underlying strengths or weaknesses of the Club's financial state at any point in time. However, as the author does not have access to all the necessary supporting historic data, it would be misleading and possibly erroneous to attempt to analyse how and why movements in fixed and current assets, current liabilities, accumulated funds, etc, have occurred over the years. Suffice it to say that even from a superficial inspection of the published accounts, it is apparent that the Club's affairs have been managed with prudence and professionalism for which all credit is due to our Honorary Treasurers and to the direction they received from the Captains and Committees of the day.

This having been said, in other chapters some background information is given as to how certain major expenditures, e.g. the purchase of the

Club, extensions to the clubhouse, etc, were financed, so these matters have not been entirely neglected.

Finally, it would be less than fair not to mention some of the more recent Club Treasurers by name. Over the last thirty years this onerous and time-consuming task has been undertaken by just five stalwarts, Messrs A. E. C. Hartnell, T. A. W. Rouse, S. J. Chubb, A. J. Mallinson, and the present incumbent, K. W. Samuda – our thanks are due to these gentlemen.

Income and Expenditure for Selected Years

As at 31st March of the year in question

Income

	Subs	*Gross Profit on Bar*	*Green Fees*	*Fruit Machines*	*Entrance Fees*	*Catering, Functions, etc*
	£	£	£	£	£	£
1955	3,758	1,555	530	—	—	—
1965	8,208	2,900	1,830	—	—	—
1975	26,170	6,385	4,497	2,000	1,189	(1,746)
1985	101,304	35,453	30,598	14,089	5,502	(3,390)
1986	110,954	39,072	36,805	14,705	7,279	(2,949)

Expenditure

	Upkeep of Course	*House Expenses*	*Other Expenses*	*Surplus/(Deficit)*
	£	£	£	£
1955	1,899	1,794	2,042	260
1965	3,647	5,811	13,561	591
1975	12,833	12,564	9,968	3,130
1985	60,206	56,671	53,056	13,623
1986	67,469	66,427	58,453	13,517

CHAPTER 14

THE LADIES' SECTION

This chapter is of necessity rather brief. Firstly, because much of what is written elsewhere in this book is no less applicable to the ladies than to the men in that it concerns the Club as a whole and all its members of both sexes and all ages. Secondly, the ladies, with a few exceptions, have been somewhat reticent in coming forward to the author with their comments and reminiscences. But for all that no-one should underestimate the contribution that the Ladies' Section has made over the years, financially, socially, and not least of all on the course itself.

Although ladies were entitled, indeed encouraged, to join the Club as playing members from its inception for a yearly subscription in 1895 of $1\frac{1}{2}$ guineas, it was not until some years later, in 1906, that they formed their own separate Ladies' Section to run and administer their own affairs. And for many years thereafter they received no financial assistance whatsoever from the Club in regard to the costs of administering their Section. A list of the Section's Captains since 1906 is given at the end of this chapter. Unlike the men, the Lady Captains' terms of office are on a calendar basis rather than from June to June.

It has always been a thriving Section and has had a number of fine golfers among its members over the years, including at least two county players, Mrs. Cathy Barclay and Mrs. Tess Hurlock, as well as quite a few ladies who were single figure handicap players at their golfing peak. But even the latter had to strive hard to be accepted and recognised for their ability in earlier times. For example, I am told that Mrs. Madge Picknett, who joined the Club in 1937 and who had a low single figure handicap, had to wait the best part of two years to be asked for a game! But in case this should give a false impression, there was, and still is, a particularly happy relationship between the Ladies' Section and the rest of the Club from the very beginning as evidenced by the large entries for the mixed foursomes which were, and still are, held regularly on Bank Holiday afternoons. Moreover, the freedom to inter-mingle within the clubhouse has increased immeasurably in recent years, likewise there has been an increase in various mixed social activities.

On the golf course itself, in addition to the Bank Holiday mixed Stablefords, there are mixed foursomes every Wednesday evening from April to September which are known affectionately as the 'Gruesomes', a Husbands' and Wives' Stableford competition in July, as well as a number of other mixed competitions, including matches against the juveniles and the Club's Geriatrics Golfing Society. However, probably the Celebration Cup, an annual mixed foursomes, Match Play, knockout competition, which was introduced by Freddie Pyrke in 1958 to 'celebrate' the purchase of the Club, is the highlight of these mixed golfing events.

Naturally, the Ladies' Section has a number of competitions and trophies of its own which are played for regularly during the season in addition, of course, to the Monthly Medal. These include:

Foxwell Bowl – which has been competed for since 1899 and is the Section's oldest extant trophy. It was presented to the Club by Mrs. Percy Foxwell who was one of the Club's original lady members. The first winner of it was Mrs. Ada Douetil, the first Captain (1906) of the Ladies' Section whose husband was a founder member and Club Captain in 1904. The inaugural competition was held on 16th May, 1899, when Mrs. Douetil scored 118–34 = 84. It more recent times the Foxwell Bowl has been the prize for the best handicap score for the Silver Division at the Section's Autumn Meeting.

Evelyn Tate Salver – presented by Evelyn Tate, a member of the famous Tate (and Lyle) sugar families. Miss Tate was the L.G.U. Manager who for many years dealt with the handicaps of Surbiton and six other clubs. In this regard, members of the Ladies' Section are not only subject to the Club's Rules but also those of the Ladies' Golf Union which set each member's handicap according to a strict and uniform procedure. Miss Tate, who had dealt with Surbiton for so many years, was invited to present the prizes at an Autumn Meeting. She was so pleased to be asked, for the first time by any club, that she subsequently presented the Ladies' Section with this magnificent silver salver.

Barnard Bowl – presented by Mrs. May Barnard (Captain in 1938 and 1946) who quite incredibly was still playing a mean game of golf at the age of 90 – try and beat that you men! May received some national press coverage for this feat at that time.

And there are other trophies such as:

Avis Trophy – presented by Hugh Avis in memory of his wife Hilda. This is a 36 hole Medal (scratch) competition.

Joan Bennet Cup – the best Medal score by a 'granny' in the Spring Meeting.

Birthday Cup – presented by Mrs. Sybil Middleton on the occasion of her 50th birthday and only eligible to ladies of that age and over; a Match Play competition.

Cochran Handicap Trophy - presented by Mrs. Erif Cochran and awarded to the lady who reduces her handicap by the greatest amount in any one year.

Grace Cup - presented by Mrs. Hilary Grace, a past Captain (1970) - a Match Play winter competition.

Mrs. Mould's Goblets - known affectionately as the 'mouldy goblets' and are the prize for the best handicap score in the Bronze Division. Mrs. Mould has the distinction of having been the Ladies' Captain for five consecutive years (1907–1911) and was, like her husband, a founder member; they were both competent golfers.

Hospital Cup - at one time all proceeds from this Medal Play competition went to London hospitals, subsequently to Surbiton Hospital or to a charity nominated by the Captain of the day.

Wernham Spoon - presented by Bryan Wernham's daughter. He had the spoon mounted as it was the only Medal spoon won by his wife, Tony, before she died. The Spoon is awarded to the winner of the Section's Mini-League.

There are at present twelve other trophies - Hilda Lovegrove Trophy, Holmes Cup, Kinnock Cups, Mrs. Knight's Cup, Captain's Prize, Captain's Trophy, Medallists' Trophy, Muriel Hamilton Trophy, NSCR Competition, Playing Fields Shield, Shearn Trophy and Surrey Fund - competed for regularly and thus the above is just a representative selection.

A few words about the course the ladies play. Currently, it measures 5,435 yards (par 71, S.S.S. 70) with an out half of 2,817 yards (par 35) and an in half of 2,618 yards (par 36). There are four holes of 400 yards or more - the 12th (458), the 14th (441), the 16th (400) and the 18th (427 yards), all of which are par-5s. It is a pretty demanding course for the average lady golfer, especially some of the long par-4s like the 1st (382 yards), the 6th (361) and the 3rd (359). Who actually holds the Ladies' course record is lost, at least to me, in the mists of time, but in 1970 the then record was equalled by a Mrs. Roberts of St. George's Hill G.C. who scored a gross 71 (net 70).

One example of several tangible contributions that the ladies have made to the Club is the unstinting way they contributed in their own right to the purchase of 'A' Notes in 1957, when, as discussed in an earlier chapter, the Club faced extinction. Nearly 50 lady members subscribed, and while quite a few of them were wives of full members, others were not. Either way they expressed their independent concern and support to the Club, and without their support the necessary sum of money would most probably not have been raised. Another example is the way they rallied round in the war years to keep the

Club going by helping to repair war damage to the course and clubhouse, providing refreshments and so on. For all these and their many other efforts over the years, the Club can be justly proud of, and grateful to, its lady members. In this regard, it is pleasing to note that five ladies – Mesdames Bennett, Hynes, Lester, Minto and Picknett – are currently Honorary Members.

Reference was made earlier to some of the fine golfers who were members in past years. In this connection it is appropriate to record that after a nine-year interval, when Mrs. Sylvia Langford was the Section's last single figure handicap (9), two ladies, Mrs. Audrey Cartwright, followed a few days later (in October 1986) by Mrs. Gwen Rice, who will be the Ladies' Captain for 1987, both achieved the distinction of becoming single figure handicap players. At the risk of being lynched by my male colleagues, I am of the opinion that the L.G.U. handicap system for ladies is somewhat more stringent and demanding in its requirements to realise and maintain a handicap for the average lady player than the more in-house method that most golf clubs apply to their men members. Whether this is true or not, it is no mean achievement for men or ladies to get down to single figures, and it is to be hoped that more ladies will join Mesdames Cartwright and Rice in the not too distant future.

Another example from recent years of the golfing quality of the Section is the success achieved by Mesdames V. M. Bell and M. Hauldron in winning the Regional Final of the Volkswagen Grand Prix Open Amateur Golf Championship in 1983. Evidence of this is to be found in the Ladies' Lounge where the trophy, a large and attractive cut-glass, stylised golf ball mounted on a plinth, is on display.

Let me conclude this chapter with one news item that caught my eye recently; it was a hole in one by Mrs. Zillah Hunt. This she achieved in February 1986 at the 107 yard 13th hole, and is illustrative of the ladies' ability to drop them straight in the hole from time to time even though the odds against doing so for the average amateur golfer are estimated to be about 43,000 to 1. In all fairness I should record that Miss Phyllis Male and Mrs. Ginny Bell also registered holes in one in 1986. Like the men, the ladies also have a hole in one trophy. This is a silver salver which was presented to the Ladies' Section by Mrs. G. W. Bennett in 1972. Engraved on it, covering the period up to the end of 1985, are fifteen names, or to be more precise fourteen names as Mrs. K. Hutchinson's name appears twice. As to be expected, most of these have been registered on the 13th, but holes in one have also been achieved on the 4th and the 11th – what about the 15th and the 17th ladies?

Finally, and to repeat, although this particular account is somewhat brief, I am greatly indebted to some lady members for much of what is recorded more appropriately elsewhere – thank you. Long may the Ladies' Section flourish.

LADY CAPTAINS

1906	Mrs. A. Douetil	1951	Mrs. T. I. Hurlock
1907	Mrs. H. J. Mould	1952	Mrs. A. Rosser
1908	Mrs. H. J. Mould	1953	Mrs. A. J. Albright
1909	Mrs. H. J. Mould	1954	Mrs. A. J. Albright
1910	Mrs. H. J. Mould	1955	Mrs. L. E. Challis
1911	Mrs. H. J. Mould	1956	Mrs. M. Hamilton
1912	Mrs. Schonberger	1957	Mrs. F. E. Pyrke
1913	Mrs. F. Richie	1958	Mrs. W. Adams
1914	Mrs. A. Douetil	1959	Mrs. J. S. Inglis
1915–18	Mrs. Arnold Hill	1960	Mrs. J. S. Inglis
1919	Mrs. R. Large	1961	Miss B. Cowderoy
1920	Mrs. H. J. Hill	1962	Mrs. D. M. Hynes
1921	Mrs. A. Eldridge	1963	Mrs. B. Marsh
1922	Mrs. A. Eldridge	1964	Mrs. P. Robertson
1923	Mrs. C. Quitman	1965	Mrs. P. Hurst
1924	Mrs. S. Vial	1966	Mrs. M. Laskey
1925	Mrs. H. Kidson	1967	Mrs. C. B. Mills
1926	Mrs. A. Eldridge	1968	Mrs. A. J. Brewis
1927	Miss Julia Hill	1969	Mrs. E. Rubenstein
1928	Mrs. A. L. Sharpe	1970	Mrs. H. Grace
1929	Mrs. S. J. Holford	1971	Mrs. P. F. C. Weeks
1930	Miss M. Overton-Jones	1972	Mrs. A. Craig
1931	Mrs. A. J. Sturgeon	1973	Mrs. G. Milne
1932	Miss W. Stevenson	1974	Mrs. L. M. Thurley
1933	Miss W. Stevenson	1975	Mrs. J. W. T. Pretsell
1934	Mrs. F. M. Betts	1976	Mrs. S. W. Norris
1935	Mrs. F. M. Betts	1977	Mrs. T. F. Prince
1936	Miss Julie Hill	1978	Mrs. A. J. Doig
1937	Mrs. J. S. Inglis	1979	Mrs. J. A. Morgan
1938	Mrs. W. J. Barnard	1980	Mrs. J. Avis
1939	Mrs. A. L. Sharpe	1981	Mrs. E. Pegler & Mrs. E. P. Holmes
1945	Mrs. S. N. Picknett		
1946	Mrs. W. J. Barnard	1982	Mrs. J. W. T. Pretsell
1947	Mrs. H. L. Moore	1983	Mrs. E. M. Kinnock
1948	Mrs. J. S. Inglis	1984	Mrs. J. Buckland
1949	Mrs. M. Kapaan	1985	Mrs. Z. Gee
1950	Mrs. L. E. Challis	1986	Mrs. E. Ramage

N.B. Some of the initials of the above Captains are those of their husbands and not their own, a long established custom which is now slowly changing as indeed it should.

CHAPTER 15

MISCELLANY

A Snippet from the Thirties

The 26th July, 1933, edition of *The Tatler* magazine contained a cartoon featuring the following members and staff:

- — Arthur J. Sturgeon, the then Captain who was also Captain the previous year;
- — S. J. 'Tod' Holford, Captain in 1916;
- — Charles H. Shuter, Captain in 1928;
- — Committee Members Eric Scott, Stanley Titford, Henry Ford, and ex-Committee Member Alec Gordon;
- — members Peter Dawson, E. O. Norton and Major A. 'Tony' J. Jiminez;
- — Capt. C. E. Crowne, the Club Secretary;
- — Jim Coleman, the Club's Professional since 1914, and Mackenzie, the Club's Steward.

The text accompanying this cartoon read as follows:

> '*Surbiton Golf Club is within easy reach of Town by way of the Kingston By-Pass, off which it lies. The Club was formerly known as The Waffrons Club, taking its name from the Waffrons Farm, a lovely old house in the middle of the course, which belongs to Capt. Donald Simson who last Sunday was host to some 130 delegates of the Empire Service League to luncheon. Golf matches were played in the afternoon. The giant beech tree, which is on the side of the eighteenth fairway, is interesting from the fact that a late member of the Club expressed the wish in his Will that his ashes should be thrown under the tree because it had always been an awkward hazard to him during his lifetime, and his wish was duly carried out with due solemnity*'.

More about the beech tree mentioned above in a moment.

A Foxy Tale

One evening in the summer of 1973, Chris and Mary Bourne were playing a friendly four-ball with Fred and Edith Austin. The light was beginning to fail and they decided to play the thirteenth and cut out the Claygate loop (the 14th, 15th and 16th). As they approached the thirteenth tee coming up through the woods, they saw two foxes sitting on the banks above the bunkers guarding the green, one on each side. The fox on the right of the green immediately ran off into the woods, but the fox on the left stayed perfectly still on top of the hump.

Fred played his shot into the right-hand bunker. Chris played a seven iron and hooked it over the fox's head into the left-hand bunker. There was no reaction from the fox! Edith played her shot low but straight and the ball stopped short of the green; still no reaction! Mary then played a perfect shot into the centre of the green. The fox got up and walked leisurely across the green, picked up Mary's ball and ran off into the woods.

The Austins, with an eye to a free drink, claimed 'Rub of the Green', but after friendly persuasion conceded Rule 27(1)(a) Note 2.

A Hole in One

It is reasonable to assume that several hundred holes in one have been scored at Surbiton since the Club was founded. Many of these achieved since 1971, but by no means all of them, are recorded on the Stewart Hewson trophy. Each must have given the golfer in question immense pleasure and satisfaction. From so many I have chosen one to relate, if only because it involved one of our more senior members and was published in two golfing magazines. The following is extracted from the letters which Mr. P. C. Frost, a 5-day member from Thames Ditton, submitted to the magazines in question.

> *'On 5th August, 1985, my father, Clifford Frost, who is 78, achieved his first hole in one. This was at Surbiton's thirteenth. He was playing with his brother, aged 80, handicap 18, at the time. Clifford said that he noticed the pin was at the back of the green so he took a seven instead of his usual nine iron. It was raining quite hard at the time so he decided not to take his pipe out of his mouth as he would have had to lay it on the wet grass. He was fortunate to see the ball all the way – straight at the flag pitching ten feet or so and rolling gently up to the pin and disappearing'.*

The postscript suggests that a hole in one has never before been achieved with a lit pipe firmly clenched between the teeth!

Nationwide Fame

At approximately 8.15 p.m. on Monday 30th December, 1985, the clubhouse, the first tee and the fifteenth green were featured anonymously, more is the pity, in the first of a new Thames Television comedy series called 'All in Good Faith' starring Richard Briers, as the Reverend Philip Lambe, and Barbara Ferris, as his wife in the series.

The clubhouse looked rather imposing on the screen, as did the men's locker room, bereft as it was of its usual extraneous clobber. The trick shot filmed on the fifteenth, pretending to be the last green where Briers was required to deliberately lose the match, necessitated a considerable amount of ingenuity. This involved Brier's aimed-off pitch shot ricochetting off three trees before the specially prepared ball was drawn into the hole by a hidden magnet.

Not quite the same perhaps as being the venue for a major golfing tournament, but fleeting fame for all that.

The Beech Tree

There have been several references in this book to the beech tree that once stood to the left of the eighteenth fairway near where it dog-legs to the right. It had long since disappeared when I joined the Club, but it continues to live in the memories of many older members and if for no other reason it deserves its own special place in this book.

The old beech tree – on the left

From the earliest days of mapping by the Ordnance Survey this grand old tree was used by them as one of their trigonometric points. How old it was, no-one will now ever know, but from its height and girth it could well have been there for at least a couple of hundred years. The tree was held in great affection by most members to the point where several of them in post-war years requested that their ashes be scattered around the base of it. Even after the tree was cut down, several members' ashes were scattered over the site. Maybe this was a custom that extended back over many years, but I have no evidence to prove it.

I am told that just before the traumas of the 1950s when the Club was put up for sale by auction, the tree was badly damaged – some say it was struck by lightning, and others that it lost some of its main branches during a gale. Whatever the cause, which is not too important, many members regarded this event as a bad omen for the future of the Club. Fortunately, as recounted in an earlier chapter, their fears eventually proved to be unfounded. However, it was unfortunate that the 'wounds' the tree had suffered were not properly treated, with the result that decay set in and in due course, after professional advice had been sought, it was cut down. At that time a member offered £500 for the timber which was a tidy sum of money in those days.

Club Colours

The origin of the Club's colours, red and yellow, has vanished in the mists of time. The most plausible reason I have been given for their choice is that they are derived from the colours of the flags the Club has on its flagsticks. It is suggested that this reason is accepted in the absence of any alternative explanation.

More Tales of Coleman

A golfing lesson from Jim Coleman was relatively simple and to the point. He would show his pupils the grip and the stance, tell them to keep their left elbows straight, and then, after placing a ball by the clubhead, he would say very firmly: '*Now 'it it, go on 'it it with yer right 'and as 'ard as yer can*!' To those who complained they were slicing his remedy was simple: '*Put yer cap under yer right elbow and keep it there without it dropping while you swing*'.

Between his workshop and the shop there used to be a tiny hidden window. On some summer evenings Coleman would sit reading quietly in his workshop. He once told a couple of members that they would be surprised if they knew all the names of some members who would help themselves to balls and other items without paying unaware that he was watching them!

On one occasion during the days when the pro and his assistant cleaned members' equipment, a rather difficult member came into Coleman's shop and upended his bag tipping clubs, mud, leaves and other debris all over the floor with the words: '*I don't call these cleaned Coleman*!'.

Perennial Issues

Three issues which have excited the feelings of many members on and off in post-war years have been standards of dress in the Clubhouse, whether or not the so-called Men's Bar should be opened up to the ladies, and starting times and booking systems for general play, especially on Saturday and Sunday mornings.

Issues of this nature can seldom be resolved to everyone's satisfaction as they are essentially matters of taste, custom and personal preference which change over time, as does the composition of the Club's members. It would be foolhardy for any individual, least of all the author, to take sides on these matters, but equally this account would not be complete if they were to be omitted or ignored.

Suffice it to say that on the question of dress, suggestions from some members that the Committee should relax the rule that requires men to wear jackets and ties in the lounge and dining room have not prevailed. Nevertheless, this having been said, various Committees over the years have relaxed the rule to the point where cravats and roll-neck sweaters are now permitted in lieu of ties, and on very hot days permission can be granted on an ad hoc basis for jackets to be discarded. In this country, the need to grant this temporary concession seldom arises!

Booking times have been abandoned and reintroduced on several occasions; at time of writing the Club is in what might be described as its no booking mode. That is not to say they will not be reintroduced at some future date, time alone will tell. Starting times, and the tees from which singles and four-balls may start, have been altered frequently. No doubt they will continue to be adjusted from time to time as playing habits (and Committees) change.

Ladies' rights and privileges in any male-dominated club or similar organisation are fraught with hazards. Whether Surbiton G.C. can be regarded as being ahead or behind the times as compared with similar golf clubs, is for each individual to assess for himself or herself. One would like to think that Surbiton has so far got it about right, and that the use of the clubhouse facilities the ladies now enjoy has the support of the majority of members.

Suggestions

Some of the suggestions that have been put to the Committee by Club members have already been touched upon earlier. The following are some further extracts from the Club's current Suggestion Book which was presented to the Club by Percy Beer when he was Captain in 1965/66. If nothing else, the Suggestion Book acts as a safety valve for members to get immediate problems off their chests, while at the same time it helps to keep the Committee on its toes and alert to the concerns of members. The suggestions are seldom earth-shaking, and with the passage of time some of them may indeed appear rather trivial in hindsight, but at the time they were made that was not necessarily the case.

May 1967 — 'We the undersigned (65 signatories) are most concerned at the influx of members of the Ladies' Section into the Men's Bar on Sunday last (lunch time and evening) . . . With ladies appearing in the Men's Bar the only area of the clubhouse allocated to men would be the locker room. We therefore look to the Committee to maintain the traditional sanctity of the Men's Bar, thus ensuring the reasonable right of the very large male membership to participate in 'male only' company when they so wish'

September 1967 'I noticed a dog being allowed to drink from a goblet which would be used later for members to drink from. I think this is unsanitary and should be forbidden'

The answer was superb:

'Agreed. This dog is being watched'.

December 1967 'I witnessed a team of horses galloping across and ruining the 8th and 18th greens . . . Are we to stand by and watch our fine course . . . hacked beyond repair?'

February 1968 'That the Club institutes a hole in one insurance'

July 1968 'Could a bell be fitted so that members could summon the steward from the terrace on hot days'

October 1968 'I found deep footmarks in two bunkers . . . this is most thoughtless on the part of the player at fault. Would it help if a short rake was available at each bunker?'

November 1968 'Chicken manure on the bank of the 7th fairway is seeping onto the course'

February 1969 'That the water on the right of the second green, now dirty, be changed!'

November 1970 'That all flag sticks be painted white the whole length'

August 1972 'Suggest the shower curtains are replaced every 10 years instead of 20!'

March 1973 'I cannot see the point in spending £8,000 on a sprinkler system and then not using it when the driest winter and earliest spring for years happens!'

March 1973 'It is suggested that the bottom of the flag sticks be painted in a contrasting colour in order that the distance from the front of the green to the hole may be more readily identified'

October 1973 'I feel that in order to encourage David Hyde the Club should extend to him the privilege of playing off the back tees!'

October 1973 'Will the Committee give sympathetic consideration to allowing members over 65 (ladies 60) and those with a physical disability, to use their trolleys during the winter months!'

May 1974 'It is suggested that to ease congestion on Medal mornings, golfers up to 12 handicap start off the first tee, while golfers over 12 handicap start off the ninth tee'

September 1974 'Why do we not have a Stag Party evening sing song around a piano? There are a number of people prepared to sing. Where is the piano?'

March 1975 'Most of the slow play on this course is caused by 'golfers' who have no knowledge or ability at the game'

'The undersigned veterans would appreciate the therapeutic value of hot water in the showers, now and then'

April 1975 'The undersigned would like to suggest that consideration be given to the provision on the course of multi-coloured flag sticks'

August 1975 'That the chairs and carpet in the men's lounge be cleaned regularly'

March 1976 'May we in future have all Medal scores listed on the notice board instead of the winner and runners-up only'

November 1976 'Would the Greens Committee consider placing the mat on the 17th hole on the high tee above the ladies' tee as this is a greatly improved 'short hole' from this position?'

February 1977 'I suggest that the Club purchase a pool or snooker table – excellent entertainment on long winter evenings'

November 1977 'Would the Committee ensure that Peter Chapman continues as assistant professional on the appointment of the new professional?'

May 1978 'In view of the swarm of would-be caddies at the clubhouse door, I suggest that the professional should be given the sole right to provide caddies and thereby maintain a greater degree of control'

July 1979 'With reference to the suggestion of the 21.5.78 and the now ever increasing swarm of would-be caddies in and around the clubhouse, has the Committee now decided on ways and means of control?'

September 1979 'Drinking in the Club swells the Club's profits. Drinking without food (or snacks) is only conducive to drunkenness. Despite repeated requests, any Club member staying on at the Club to drink and swell the Club's profits, cannot get anything to eat after approx. 5.30 p.m. except for a limited number of toasted sandwiches. Can we therefore please have a supply of peanuts, cheese biscuits, crisps or the like, available for purchase at any time from the bar?'

July 1980 'Would appreciate a 'fountain of water' for drink-ing just outside the first tee'

August 1980 'Re cheese biscuits and peanuts (September 1979), these are still not available for sale!'

Early 1981 'The undersigned would wish to congratulate the new head greenkeeper on the improvements already made to the course and we wish him success in the future'

'Would appreciate a fountain of drinking water just outside the first tee'

Winter 1983 'Could the winter greens be clearly marked out with white lines to stop people inadvertently walking with trolleys over them?'

January 1984 'I suggest that the greens staff be instructed to revert to the previous practice to place two flags on the flag stick at all times when the hole is situated on the upper level of the 9th green'

March 1984 'Over the years tens of thousands of pounds have been spent on the clubhouse. Would it be possible to spend a few hundred on wire fencing to keep the constant herd of animals off our course which cause so much damage . . . this problem has been with us for at least the last 20 years!'

June 1985 'It was clear to the members that attended the AGM last night that the majority of those present wished to see more competitive golf played in the Club. With this in mind, it is suggested that the Club organise and run an official fourball league this coming winter'

October 1985 'I would like to suggest that some control is exercised over the numbers and quality of visiting golfers who play at S.G.C. I would not presume to suggest what these controls might be, but I would like to mention that in my opinion the situation has deteriorated to a level which is now unacceptable. I do believe that each golfer should have a set of clubs, should have some basic knowledge of the etiquette of the game and, preferably, should have played before'

To repeat, the above are but a representative selection irrespective of their merits. Omitted are the many suggestions relating to the course itself such as the repositioning of tees, alternative layouts for some holes, course maintenance matters and the like. Also omitted, quite deliberately, are the Committee's response to these suggestions as I thought that readers might wish to ponder for themselves how they would have responded had they been a Committee Member at the times in question.

What a pity the Suggestion Book(s) of earlier years no longer exists, this would probably have made rather more fascinating reading.

Bits and Bobs

Wally Hammond, the Surrey and England cricketer, was a member around the war years, as was Petula Clark's father.

The lowest handicap ever held by a Club member, at least as far as I have been able to trace, was plus 3. This handicap was held by a Mr. R. Large in the years before the Great War. With a net higher than his gross score, his best performance in a Monthly Medal was to come third – its tough at the top.

In the Club's early days, gaining membership was largely a function of one's standing in society, playing ability counted for little; lesser mortals tended to join Claygate Common Golf Club or other nearby clubs that had artisan sections, Surbiton didn't.

Laurence Ide spent so much time in the 1950s working on and about the course that when he was persuaded eventually to stand for the Committee (elected in 1959) many members thought he was one of the ground staff.

For those who think they are rather good putters, did you know that the record for the fewest putts over 18 holes is 14 by Colin Collen-

Smith at Betchworth Park, Dorking, in 1947? He chipped into the hole four times and single putted the remaining 14 greens.

The present pro's shop and trolley shed were built in 1965.

Life in any club does not run smoothly all the time. In October 1976, over 30 full men members called an Extraordinary General Meeting in accordance with Rule 15. At the EGM on the 26th, the resolution put to the meeting – a vote of no confidence in the elected General Committee – was defeated by 120 votes to 15 with 15 abstentions.

The handsome Club sign carved on a tree trunk that is located on the north side of the clubhouse close to the first tee, was made and presented to the Club by Messrs. N. Pack and R. Dudman in 1986.

In May 1986, three of the Club's juvenile members, R. Blunden, C. Cowper and J. Cameron, raised £700 for Sports Aid by completing 100 holes in one day. A splendid achievement which was almost, but not quite, a Club record in that during the last war two members managed to complete six rounds (108 holes) in one day.

Up until 1967, all holes, except of course the par-3s, had fairway markers sited 200 yards from the tees.

Attempts by some members during the late 1960s/early 1970s to persuade the Committee to put a colour TV set in the mixed lounge were unsuccessful; it was not until 1977 that a set was eventually installed.

In the winter of 1968/69 some members suggested that the diameter of the holes on temporary greens should be increased to 6 inches as this would make the game 'much more enjoyable'. Needless to say the suggestion was not accepted. Even so many of us today would welcome larger sized holes all the year round!

Golf courses are designed basically for right-handed players. This has led to a number of requests over the years from left-handed players for trees to be cut back around several tees in order not to put them at an unnecessary disadvantage. But trees grow and Greens Committees cannot always remember the needs of our cack-handed brethren.

Enough is enough – this concludes my version of the history of Surbiton Golf Club. In spite of its omissions, incompleteness, inaccuracies and other imperfections, I hope the reader will have found a few things in it of interest to him or her.

Once again, my sincere thanks to all those who helped to make this book possible, and particularly to Gilbert Fuge and Don Blanchard for their support and encouragement throughout its preparation. Finally, forget not the six Ss – swing slowly, swing smoothly, swing sweetly, and the Monthly Medal is yours for the taking.

SELECTED REFERENCES

The following is a selection of the principal references consulted by the author. These were supplemented by members' recollections and correspondence from various parties with the Club. Where apparent inconsistencies and discrepancies existed, the author selected what he considered to be the most reliable/accurate source of information. For ease of reading and comprehension, no attempt has been made to litter the text with a multiplicity of references.

Apportionment of the Rent Charge in Lieu of Tithes in the Parish of Thames Ditton: Agreement for the Commutation of Tithes, 1843.

Benson and Hedges Golfer's Handbook 1985, edited by Laurence Viney, Macmillan London Ltd., 1985.

Burnett, Bobby, Historian of The Royal & Ancient Golf Club of St. Andrews, various material.

Cornish & Whitton, *The Golf Course*, Ellesborough Press.

Cousins, Geoffrey, *Golf in Britain*, Routledge & Kegan Paul, 1975.

Cruickshank, Charles, *The History of Royal Wimbledon Golf Club 1865–1986*, Royal Wimbledon G.C., 1986.

Encyclopedia of Golf, compiled by Webster Evans, Robert Hale & Co., 1974.

Golf (a journal), various editions.

Golfing Annual, 1895, 1896 and *1897* editions, publisher not known.

Golfing Illustrated (a journal), Brand Publishing Ltd., various editions.

Golf World (a journal), various editions.

Henderson, Ian T. and Stirk, David I., *The Compleat Golfer*, Victor Gollancz, 1982.

Hutchinson, Horace G., *British Golf Links*, J. S. Virtue & Co. Ltd., 1897.

Hutchinson, Horace G., *Famous Golf Links*, Longmans, Green & Co., 1891.

Kelly's Directory of Kingston, Surbiton, Esher and district, various editions.

Leases of various dates entered into by the Trustees of Surbiton Golf Club.

Lovelace Estate papers.

McDonnell, Michael, *The Complete Book of Golf*, Kingswood Press, 1985.

Peebles, Malcolm W. H., *The Claygate Book*, Malcolm Peebles, 1983.

Rees, Dai, *Thirty Years of Championship Golf*, Stanley Paul, 1968.
Surbiton Golf Club, Annual Reports, Accounts and Minutes of AGMs and EGMs, 1956–1986.
Surbiton Golf Club, Suggestion Book, 1966–1986.
Surbiton Golf Club Limited, Notices and Minutes of various AGMs.
Surrey Comet (a newspaper), various editions.
Surrey County Magazine (a journal), various editions.
Victoria History of the County of Surrey, edited by H. E. Malden, Archibald Constable & Co. Ltd., 1905.
Who Was Who, 1929–1940, Adam & Charles Black, 1947.

The course, or at least a part of it, making its contribution to the war effort

SUBSCRIBERS

The following lists, in order of receipt, those individuals whose subscriptions to this book were received by end of July 1987, when this list went to print. Their support in advance of publication is much appreciated and has helped in no small way to make it possible to publish this book.

1 H. C. Judd, Esher
2 Mrs H. Grace, Esher
3 M. J. Bice, Chessington
4 R. W. J. Vincent, Claygate
5 Mrs C. M. Hewson, Cheam
6 B. J. Lester, Walton-on-Thames
7 B. C. Munro, Claygate
8 P. I. Griffiths, Teddington
9 N. J. Duffell, Worcester Park
10 G. T. Fuge, O.B.E., Cobham
11 G. T. Fuge, O.B.E., Cobham
12 P. D. Keeler, Hinchley Wood
13 D. B. Newman, Petersham
14 B. R. Pettitt, East Ewell
15 J. N. Weatherall, London SW15
16 L. J. Lando, Hinchley Wood
17 H. Paton Evans, Esher
18 A. Craig, Swanage
19 R. A. Beardon, Worcester Park
20 M. H. Spearing, Claygate
21 Mrs C. Bettinson, Berrylands
22 H. E. Green, Ewell
23 B. E. Green, Ewell
24 M. E. Pearce, Leatherhead
25 Mrs C. Minto, Weybridge
26 G. J. Mellalieu, Chessington
27 K. A. Pegler, New Malden
28 W. R. Hall, Banstead
29 F. W. Mills, Claygate
30 J. Andrews, Chessington
31 P. A. Browne, Chessington
32 D. T. Blanchard, Surbiton
33 J. G. Ottaway, Walton-on-Thames
34 T. W. Blackmore, Morden
35 P. N. Donne-Davis, Claygate
36 R. F. Willson, Cheam
37 I. R. P. Arthur, Cobham
38 E. J. Enderby, Ewell
39 J. Lee, Oxshott
40 T. M. Merchant, Worcester Park
41 D. J. P. Wordsworth, East Molesey
42 C. T. Bourne, Oxshott
43 J. A. Jinks, Chessington
44 J. A. H. Ayris, Cheam
45 R. E. Baker, Claygate
46 G. S. Mallinson, Cobham
47 A. E. Weston, Wimbledon Park
48 J. Simpson, Chessington
49 B. D. Bantin, Claygate
50 R. W. Martin, Shepperton
51 W. P. Beer, Kingston-on-Thames
52 A. McGinn, Claygate
53 Mrs O. C. Grumbar, Worcester Park
54 Mrs Z. Gee, Claygate
55 W. H. G. Kinnock, Ditton
56 J. T. Cook, Walton-on-the-Hill
57 Mrs J. White, West Ewell
58 F. I. Valentine, Claygate
59 Mrs M. D. Hynes, Thames Ditton
60 W. C. Farenden, Claygate
61 D. R. Farenden, Claygate
62 W. R. T. Pick, Claygate
63 N. J. Pimm, Claygate
64 Mrs E. Bryant, Worthing
65 R. R. Bryant, Worthing
66 K. C. Green, Cobham
67 C. R. Brenchley, Claygate
68 W. T. McMahon, Surbiton
69 R. B. McCall, Ewell
70 A. E. K. Webber, Ilford
71 C. A. Pink, Esher
72 S. W. Tickner, Surbiton
73 F. W. Girling, Surbiton
74 L. R. Haskett, Claygate
75 G. A. Huard, Ealing
76 P. E. Norden, West Ewell
77 A. G. Hillier, Surbiton
78 J. A. Black, Sutton
79 P. J. O'Dwyer, Weston Green
80 D. Allan, Esher
81 D. Allan, Esher
82 R. L. Harrison, Cobham
83 G. A. de Jonge, Claygate
84 D. R. C. Munro, Reigate
85 J. E. Harper, Surbiton
86 M. K. Pearce, East Molesey
87 I. P. Sunley, New Malden
88 Mrs E. E. Bradley, Esher

89 L. Barnes, Worcester Park
90 E. A. Hughes, West Wimbledon
91 E. D. Peacock, Surbiton
92 D. R. Vallance, Worcester Park
93 R. Forgan, Chessington
94 B. J. Hauldren, Claygate
95 P. M. O'Connell, Claygate
96 P. F. C. Weeks, Weybridge
97 F. Carter, Claygate
98 J. D. Adams, Morden
99 Mrs M. J. Saggs, Thames Ditton
100 M. R. A. Nicholls, Claygate
101 M. R. A. Nicholls, Claygate
102 M. K. Nordemann, Claygate
103 M. E. R. Thornhill, Thames Ditton
104 P. R. Ekeberg, Esher
105 A. W. Bowyer, Claygate
106 D. J. Elvidge, Chessington
107 J. H. Denyer, Bournemouth
108 P. L. Barnes, Thames Ditton
109 J. Eastman, Claygate
110 M. K. Webster, Chessington
111 J. R. Camp, Epsom
112 L. C. Clews, Chessington
113 P. B. Quinlan, Wimbledon Park
114 Mrs S. W. Norrie, Weybridge
115 Mrs M. F. Robertson, Hinchley Wood
116 W. Fotheringham, Cobham
117 F. C. Markey, West Wickham
118 A. L. Lytton, Surbiton
119 Mrs E. B. Ramage, Hinchley Wood
120 W. M. Carnie, Surbiton
121 Mrs G. Rice, Hinchley Wood
122 Dr J. W. T. Pretsell, Surbiton
123 A. G. E. Stackwood, Hinchley Wood
124 R. H. Avis, Corfe Castle
125 F. J. Timothy Pyrke, Putney
126 T. Simon Pyrke, Putney
127 Mrs B. W. Brady, Llandudno Gwynedd
128 B. J. Jeffries, Hampton
129 P. C. J. Havelock, Claygate
130 Mrs A. D. Cartwright, Claygate
131 A. Downing, Kingston-upon-Thames
132 J. D. K. Crommelin, Claygate
133 N. Upson, Surbiton
134 M. L. Green, Claygate
135 A. E. Smith, Surbiton Golf Club
136 F. J. Burton, Tolworth
137 A. C. Bonfield, Hinchley Wood
138 C. R. G. Young, Leatherhead
139 Mrs. E. A. O'Neill, Hersham
140 I. D. Cameron, Esher
141 J. M. Crichton, Cobham
142 D. W. Redpath, Esher
143 C. M. Philimore, Hindhead
144 P. A. Bloxham, Surbiton
145 A. Todd, Maidenhead
146 J. A. Kemp, West Molesey
147 M. B. Casey, London W8
148 M. D. Wright, Surbiton Golf Club
149 D. A. Lonie, Weston Green